Baucom—TOTAL COMMUNICATION USED IN
EXPERIENCE BASED SPEECHREADING
AND AUDITORY TRAINING LESSON PLANS

Publication Date: 1-2-81
Price: cloth–$12.50, paper–$7.75

THIS BOOK IS BEING SENT TO YOU

FOR REVIEW

IN

DSH ABSTRACTS

BY

CHARLES C THOMAS, *Publisher*

301-327 EAST LAWRENCE AVENUE

SPRINGFIELD, ILLINOIS 62717 • U.S.A.

IF A REVIEW APPEARS, WE SHOULD APPRECIATE

BEING SENT TWO COPIES FOR

OUR FILES

Total Communication Used in Experience Based Speechreading and Auditory Training Lesson Plans

Total Communication Used in Experience Based Speechreading and Auditory Training Lesson Plans

FOR HARD OF HEARING AND DEAF INDIVIDUALS

By

MARTA E. BAUCOM, M.Ed.

Audiologist and Speech-Language Pathologist
Guilford County Health Department
Greensboro, North Carolina

and

RALPH E. CAUSBY, M.S.

Instructor in Education of the Deaf
and Audiologist
University of North Carolina at Greensboro
Greensboro, North Carolina

CHARLES C THOMAS • **PUBLISHER**
Springfield • Illinois • U.S.A.

Published and Distributed Throughout the World by
CHARLES C THOMAS ● PUBLISHER
Bannerstone House
301-327 East Lawrence Avenue, Springfield, Illinois, U.S.A.

With THOMAS BOOKS *careful attention is given to all details of
manufacturing and design. It is the Publisher's desire to present books that
are satisfactory as to their physical qualities and artistic possibilities and
appropriate for their particular use.* THOMAS BOOKS *will be true to those
laws of quality that assure a good name and good will.*

Printed in the United States of America
V-R-1

Library of Congress Cataloging in Publication Data

Baucom, Marta E
  Total communication used in experience based
speechreading and auditory training lesson plans.

  Bibliography: p.
  Includes index.
  1. Deaf--Means of communication. I. Causby,
Ralph E., joint author. II. Title. [DNLM:
1. Rehabilitation. 2. Lip reading. 3. Deafness--
Rehabilitation. 4. Hearing loss, Partial--Rehabilita-
tion. 5. Education, Special. HV2483 B337t]
HV2471.B38   371.91'27   80-18518
ISBN 0-398-04124-5
ISBN 0-398-04125-3 (pbk.)

In Memory Of

HOWARD ATLAS BAUCOM
WILLIAM THOMAS CAUSBY

ACKNOWLEDGMENTS

THE authors wish to express special thanks to students enrolled in Aural Rehabilitation classes (1976-1979) for their assistance in preparation of the lesson plans presented in this book.

M.E.B.
R.E.C.

CONTENTS

                                                                    Page

Acknowledgments vii

Chapter

1. INTRODUCTION 3
2. METHODS USED IN DEVELOPING THE EXPERIENCE
      BASED PLANS.. 12
3. PROCEDURE FOR ALL PLANS............................. 16
4. PRESCHOOL LESSON PLANS 21
5. LESSON PLANS FOR SCHOOL AGE CHILDREN............... 30
6. ADULT LESSON PLANS 87
7. SUGGESTIONS FOR DEVELOPING ADDITIONAL PLANS......... 124
8. DATA COLLECTION 127

Appendix

   A. Interviews — Adult 129
   B. Interviews — Children.......................... 139
   C. The Visible Components of the Speech Sounds...... 142
   Bibliography....................................... 145
   Index.. 147

Total Communication Used in Experience Based Speechreading and Auditory Training Lesson Plans

Chapter 1

INTRODUCTION

REVIEW OF OLDER SPEECHREADING MATERIAL

$\mathbf{A}$ REVIEW of the Bruhn, Jena, Nitchie, and Kinzie speechreading materials dating to the 1900s shows that a need exists for plans that are experience based, logically organized, and compatible with a Total Communication program. Alice Streng summarized these older, extensively used methods, and the authors feel that her summary, which follows, is detailed enough to illustrate that new materials are needed.*

According to Streng (1969, p. 197), Martha Bruhn translated the German Mueller-Walle Method and published three books. This method later became known in the United States as the Bruhn Method. Bruhn acknowledged the need of synthetic power for the speechreader but felt "that the student must be aware of and be able to analyze details" (1969, p. 197). She introduced each lesson with a description of the movement and used rapid rhythmic syllable drills to teach the student to analyze details. In the first lesson she combines the visible consonants /p/, /b/, /m/; /s/, /z/; /f/, /v/; /sh/, /ch/, /th/; and /w/, /wh/ with vowels into syllables such as (fō), (fä), etc. The drills are presented in rhythmic patterns and lead into paradigms which are expanded into sentences. Bruhn's lessons include stories that are developed through phrases and sentences, and the lessons conclude with homophenous drills and written work.

The Jena Method, as reviewed by Streng (1969, p. 198), shows that the method was devised by Karl Brauckmann in Jena, Germany, and was introduced into the United States by Jacob Reighard and Bessie Whitaker. Details of the method were published in the United States in 1932 by Anna Bunger in

---

*Adapted from Alice Streng, *Hearing Therapy for Children*, 2d edition, 1969, pp. 197-201. By permission of Grune & Stratton, New York.

3

Speechreading-Jena Method. The Jena Method proposes that of the five forms of speech, the movement form is the most important to the speechreader. It assumes that if the speechreader can unconsciously reproduce the speech movements of the speaker on his own lips, he will possess one of the best tools for interpreting speech. Therefore, the aim of the Jena Method "is to develop kinesthetic awareness of speech" (Streng, 1969, p. 199). Streng (1969, p. 199) reports that in the Jena Method, the speechreader must memorize the following vowel series: "ā, ē, ō, ah, aw, ĕ, ōō, ă, ū, ou, ī, oi, ŏo, ĭ, ŭ, er." In the Jena Method vowels are combined with consonants into syllables and presented in several different rhythm patterns. The rhythm patterns are reinforced with movements such as bouncing a ball or clapping hands (1969, p. 199). After several weeks of syllable drill training, the Jena Method advances to a synthetic approach. At the synthetic level, the lessons are designed around subjects that are of interest to the students. The lessons include sentences and stories based on biographies, current events, etc.

The Nitchie Method, as described by Streng (1969, p. 199), points out that the method was not fully developed until 1919 when Edward Nitchie's book, *Lipreading-Principles and Practices*, was published. The Nitchie Method suggests that each lesson begin with a description of the movement to be studied. His lessons generally adhere to the following format:

Description of the Movement
Practice Words
Sentences with Clue Words
Homophenous Word Drills
Idiomatic Expressions and Adages
Story

Streng (1969, p. 201) reported that the Kinzie sisters wrote two books on speechreading, *Lipreading for Deafened Adults* and *Lipreading for Children (Book I, II, and III)*, which combine the Nitchie and Bruhn Methods. The Kinzie material is based on the interest and abilities of children from the first grade through the young adult level. The first book of *Lipreading for Children* provides informal lessons such as simple stories. The second book is semiformal, and the lessons are based on movements. Each lesson in Book II includes word and sentence drills, a story exercise, rhymes, and finger play activities. The third book is formal and designed for adults. Each lesson includes a description of the movement to be studied, vowel drills, and vocabulary lists that serve as clues for sentences.

The authors agree with the following Jeffers and Barley (1971, pp. 94-111) criticisms of the Bruhn (Mueller-Walle), Jena, Nitchie, and Kinzie Methods and feel that these criticisms further support the fact that more current materials are needed.*

The primary criticism of the Bruhn Method is the use of stilted and unnatural sentences that appear in the first lessons. A further criticism is that there is no differentiation of mind training from eye training (Jeffers and Barley, 1971, p. 103).

The Jena Method is criticized for stressing kinesthetic sensations since its importance has not been established. Jeffers and Barley state that "it is obviously true that the speechreader can imitate only that portion of the message that he can see or hear, the same information that he gets without imitation. Moreover, he is just as apt to make errors as the non-imitator, if he imitates a message incorrectly. And he has the same job of mentally filling in information which he can neither see nor hear" (pp. 110-11). Jeffers and Barley also criticize the analytic approach to rhythm in teaching speechreading because there is no evidence to support its benefit (1971, p. 111).

Jeffers and Barley criticized the actual teaching materials involved in the Nitchie Method (1971, p. 99). They state, "his philosophy stressed the separation of associational materials from those designed for eye training and more emphasis being placed on training in association than on training for visibility. But unfortunately, his methods do not follow his philosophy. The associational materials consist only of a series of unrelated sentences and of short stories that are written for reading rather than for conversation. The sentence materials are based on the various movements and evolve from the eye training material rather than being separated from them" (p. 99).

The Kinzie material has been criticized at the formal level in Book III because the material at this level tends to be too stilted, and vision and hearing are not coordinated in their

---

*Adapted from Janet Jeffers and Margaret Barley, *Speechreading (Lipreading)*, 1971. By permission of Charles C Thomas, Publisher, Springfield.

teaching. The clue words are criticized because the clue is most often just a word from the sentence and does not adequately identify the sentence (1971, p. 108).

REVIEW OF OLDER AUDITORY TRAINING MATERIAL

According to Newby (1979, p. 402), auditory training before World War II was confined to teaching students enrolled in schools for the deaf to be aware of gross sounds. There were few attempts to train students to discriminate between speech sounds. One of the early methods that extended training beyond gross sound training was the Acoustic Method, which was developed by Dr. Max Goldstein at the Central Institute for the Deaf in the 1920s. Streng (1969, p. 318) described his method by stating that "he advocated the interpretation of speech by tactile and auditory impression to encompass pitch, rhythm, accent, volume and inflection."

Newby (1979, p. 402) states that "not until World War II, however, was much attention paid to the problems of teaching the hard of hearing how to make the most of their residual hearing." Newby also reports that auditory training was not practiced to any great extent until the development of wearable hearing aids. Newby (1979, p. 403) summarizes the early beginning of auditory training as an outgrowth of training at the aural rehabilitation centers operated by the armed services in World War II. He states, "In addition to classes in speech-reading and in speech conversation, a class in auditory training was developed at each of the military centers. Some included in their program a listening hour; at that time, patients would get informal practice in a variety of listening situations, thus supplementing on their own the formal instruction they received in class" (1979, p. 403).

Oyer (1966, p. 117) also reviewed older auditory training materials. His review of recorded materials includes Mary Whitehurst's *Hearing Rehabilitation Children's Series*; Breshanan and Pronovost's *Let's Listen* records; Jean Utley's *What's Its Name* album; Arthur and Elaine's *We Speak Through Music* albums; Laila L. Larsen's *Consonant Sound Discrimination* and *Recordings for Auditory Training*. Oyer's review of printed materials (1966, p. 121) included the following material by Mary W. Whitehurst:

Auditory Training Manual
Let's Travel by Way of Language
Auditory Training, Lipreading and Speech
Auditory Training for Children
Auditory Training for the Deaf
Three Stories to Hear, Color and Read

Oyer also reviewed other printed materials such as *Play It By Ear* by Lowell and Stoner, *Clinician's Handbook for Auditory Training* by James C. Kelly, *Tim and His Hearing Aid* by Ronnei and Porter, *A Manual for Auditory Training* by Louis M. DiCarlo, and other materials. Oyer's detailed accounts of these older manuals and methods may be referred to for more complete information on early training materials.

Streng (1969, p. 314) also refers to two other older methods that provide training beyond gross sound training. She described the Babbling Method by Josephine Avondino as "a method using syllable drills as the basis for teaching words, phrases or sentences." Her description of the Tadoma Method, which was devised by Kate and Sophia Alcorn, shows that vibration training was used to present the pattern of speech.

Streng (1969, p. 201) reports that one should review the older methods before attempting to design new material. However, after researching older methods, most teachers concluded that they must write their own plans if they want material that is experience based and interesting to children. Streng (1969, p. 202) states that "the unifying effect of a single subject tends to furnish some of the kinds of clues necessary to understanding speech visually." Streng's suggestions of subject based plans have been incorporated into the plans in this guide.

REVIEW OF CURRENT SPEECHREADING MATERIALS

From the writers' review of current speechreading materials such as Jeffers' and Barley's, Ena MacNutt's, Mae Fisher's, and Rose Broberg's, it is evident that all of these materials and procedures may be used successfully. They are primarily synthetic and the procedures are easily followed. However, only a few current speechreading materials center the plans on a particular topic or event that the writers feel is necessary in beginning lessons. In general, current speechreading material is seldom written in conversational style, and none of the plans reviewed make provisions for incorporating them into a Total Communication program.

REVIEW OF CURRENT AUDITORY TRAINING MATERIALS

Materials and sample lesson plans on auditory training are either nonexistent or difficult to find. In reviewing current literature on auditory training, the writers were able to find only a limited number of actual plan guides. Most books and articles reviewed presented general guidelines for training, an explanation of the human communication system, the acoustics of speech, and information on auditory training equipment and hearing aids. However, a few recent publications suggest some sample plans or guides. Streng (1969, p. 215) outlines a plan for discrimination exercises that includes recognizing likenesses, rhyming words, etc. She also shows a topic based plan that includes procedures for vocabulary development, phrase and sentence drill, and homophenous word study.

Berg and Fletcher (1970, pp. 321-23) describe an auditory training plan developed in 1951 by Erik Wedenberg for his son Staffan. It was early reported that the basis for his successful auditory training program was early identification of the hearing problem, provision for proper fitting of a hearing aid, and cooperative parents who are willing to assist in training. The Wedenberg plan suggests that "one must diminish the visual impression in order that the auditory stimuli might exercise first claim upon the consciousness" (p. 321). The training procedure according to the Wedenberg plan starts training with two vowel sounds that have first formants that are far apart. Later, other vowel sounds that have first formants that are closer together in the spectrum are added. After vowel sounds are mastered, voiced consonants with low first formants are combined with the vowels to form words. Later, unvoiced consonants are included to form words. Wedenberg noted that when unvoiced consonants were introduced, it was helpful to add tactile cues to assist in reception.

The authors have found that tactile cues aid in providing information, especially at the initial stage of auditory training, and they may be helpful in successive plans. Place cueing such as the following is helpful: (1) place the fingers to the side of the nose to feel the vibration for nasals, (2) lightly place the fingers against the side of the throat for feeling voiced consonants, (3) hold the hand in front of the mouth to feel the breath for unvoiced consonants.

Berg (1976, pp. 120-23) reviews another more current type of auditory training plan which was developed by Sister James Lorene Hogan at St. Joseph's School for the Deaf in 1961. The plan, called the *ABC's of Auditory Training*, includes gross sound discrimination training as well as speech discrimination training. Berg (1976, p. 124) states that the plan includes

> discrimination of the speech stimuli that consists of compounds like pie and coffee, ball and glove, and pen and pencil. Initally, the child looks at the instructor as she says the word; the child also utilizes auditory clues delivered by his hearing aid. The instructor shows the child the printed form so that he has a perceptual set. Then she asks him to turn away. He listens auditorially but can refer visually to the printed options or choices of responses. Then he identifies the correct stimulus. Finally, the instructor removes the structure or printed options to determine the competence of the child in discriminating auditorially between 12 stimuli including pie and coffee.*

Berg (1976, p. 127) also reviewed the Verbotonal approach, which was developed by Guberina at a school for the hearing impaired in Zagreb, Yugoslavia. Guberina's success is attributed to the use of a series of hearing aids called SUVAG. At Guberina's school, all children begin auditory training with daily use of SUVAG I, which amplifies from 0.5 to 15,000 Hz. When the child is able to respond to sound by using the SUVAG I equipment, he is advanced to training with SUVAG II. With the SUVAG II equipment the teacher is able to select

---

*From Frederick S. Berg, *Educational Audiology*, 1976. By permission of Grune & Stratton, New York.

specific intensities and frequencies at which the child is able to understand speech best. When the child is not using the SUVAG I or II equipment, he is fitted with a body model mini-SUVAG. Berg (1976, p. 127) states, "If a child has little or no residual hearing, he also receives speech and language instruction by use of an electro-tactile device or vibrator that can be coupled to the mini-SUVAG." The Verbotonal approach to auditory training is not widely used, but it is being used successfully in at least two schools for the deaf in the United States.

Sanders (1971, pp. 260-74) presents an auditory training plan that includes gross sound and speech sound discrimination training. The limited plans are topic related and appear to be in good coversational style. Sample plans are included for children as well as for adults.

Ling (1976, p. 45) reports that speech acquisition is the prime objective of auditory training and that auditory training necessitates the use of speech. His plans start at the phonetic level with nonsense syllables concentrating on the suprasegmental features of pitch, intensity, and duration. Later, these features are applied to the phonological level. Ling (1976, p. 5) further states that "manual communication is detrimental to the development of speech and spoken language." However, at recent workshops he has discussed the possibility of merging his auditory approach into the Total Communication program.

The authors combined speechreading material with auditory training material into a Total Communication approach since experience has shown that, when possible, one should not attempt to rely on speechreading alone for reception of speech. Ross (1972, p. 34) states, "Rarely does the hard of hearing person meet with communicative situations in which he is completely unable to utilize his residual hearing. Lipreading training which omits the auditory signal is not only unrealistic but may be tapping a different skill from what is required to learn to use simultaneous visual and auditory clues." He further supports the bisensory approach by reporting that one of the most reliable research findings is that hearing impaired individuals comprehend speech better with combined visual and auditory input. The auditory training and speechreading material in this guide is especially designed to be incorporated into a Cued Speech program or a Total Communication program. All material is experience based and there are plans for children as well as for adults. It is designed to be used by teachers in a residential school for the deaf, and it is applicable for individual use in a clinical setting.

Chapter 2

METHODS USED IN DEVELOPING
THE EXPERIENCE BASED PLANS

STUDENTS enrolled at the University of North Carolina at Greensboro in aural rehabilitation classes from 1976 to 1979 were asked to write experience based speech-reading lesson plans in partial fulfillment of class requirements. Some students observed or talked to children to obtain material for their plans. Other students interviewed hearing impaired adults to obtain samples of common terms used in conjunction with their profession and/or terms used in connection with hobbies, sports, etc. Adults with normal hearing were also interviewed when it was felt that their profession might be a possible employment site for a hearing impaired individual.

All interviews were recorded and were utilized by the students to design the lesson plans. For example, a young mechanical draftsman was interviewed. His first lesson was designed to include terms used in his profession, feeling that the language would be familiar to him. A high interest in the material was another assumption. In another plan a young child was interviewed, and it was learned that she enjoys dancing class. She was excited about the class and wanted to talk about it. Therefore, her first lesson was based on terms familiar to her about dancing. Several interview forms for adults and children are provided in Appendices A and B.

Students used words and terminology from the interview forms to write Quick Recognition Exercises (Q.R.E.), Quick Identification Exercises (Q.I.E.), Sentence Exercises, and Story Exercises, and when possible all material related to a single topic. Procedures detailed by Jeffers and Barley (1971, pp. 190-247) were used throughout the original plans, and no attempt was made by the students to include provisions for sign language.

The goals for each step in the lesson plans are essentially the same as the goals advocated by Jeffers and Barley (1971, pp. 190-247). The goal for Q.R.E. is to improve "visual perception and improvement in speed of perception" (1971, p. 190). The goal for Q.I.E. is to "improve retention of visual imagery and permit quick association of a pattern with the various homo-phenous words for which it serves as a cue" (1971, p. 201). The goal for Sentence Exercises is to improve training in association and to prepare the speechreader for changes in conversation. The goal of the Story Exercise is to make the speechreader less dependent on immediate knowledge, to force the speech-reader to be dependent on contextual clues, and to improve both short-term and long-term visual and verbal memory.

This present compilation of lesson plans is a result of the writers' attempt to collect all student plans and to correct the Q.R.E. and Q.I.E. Sentences and stories were added or revised by the authors to follow Streng's (1969, pp. 205-207) rules for sentences and stories. It was neither the intent nor the claim of the authors to present an exhaustive compilation of lesson plans suitable for all individual needs since it is realized that most plans must be tailored to the individual. The writers have, however, provided enough plans that are on the correct lan-guage and speechreading level for children and adults to enable a beginning therapist to construct further plans in the same form.

The authors included Total Communication in the Jeffers and Barley procedures to make the material appropriate for those individuals who have very limited residual hearing. Many profoundly deaf or deafened individuals cannot comprehend speech without the addition of sign language, and many may be unable to respond if not allowed to respond by using sign language. The writers have observed that many deaf and deaf-ened individuals need to have directions given and word meaning explained through signs prior to expecting them to speechread a word or sentence. Therefore, it is suggested that, when necessary, all instructions and explanations be given by using Total Communication and that responses other than oral ones be accepted throughout the lessons.

Therapists are cautioned about using signs too quickly with some deaf and/or deafened individuals since it has been noted that even remnants of residual hearing can be utilized when FM transmission type auditory training equipment is used.

The writers experimented with Phonic Ear (HC 421) FM type auditory trainers with the lesson plans in this guide and found that responses with FM type equipment were superior to responses obtained with wearable hearing aids. According to Phonic Ear's *Operating Instruction Guide,* the equipment is generally used in three ways:

> *Teacher Transmission Only* involves turning the mike switch to the off position with the power switch on. With this setting the individual is able to receive only sounds that are transmitted by the teacher. This enables the individual to hear the teacher's voice clearly, even when the environment is noisy.
>
> The second way to use the equipment is called *Teacher Transmission and Environmental Sounds.* For this setting the mike switch and the power switch are both turned on and the individual is able to interact with other students, hear sounds around him, monitor his own voice, and receive sound transmitted from the teacher. However, with this setting, room noise must be controlled.
>
> Another setting for the FM equipment is a setting where *Environmental Sounds only* are received. For this setting the Receiver Oscillator is removed and the mike and power switch are on. With this setting the receiver becomes a conventional binaural hearing aid. The individual receives no transmission from the teacher, but he hears his own voice and other sounds in the environment.

Best results were obtained with the lesson material outlined in this guide with the setting for Teacher Transmission and Environmental sounds when environmental noise was controlled. Therefore, it is suggested that FM type auditory training equipment be used when available rather than wearable hearing aids.

As the authors added auditory training material to the original speechreading lesson plans, careful attention was given to the design of the material. In general, each plan shows a progression from words that are easy to discriminate between to more difficult material whereby words are difficult to discriminate beween.

The auditory training material following Q.R.E. presents a one syllable word contrasted with two words or multisyllabic words. These words are easy to differentiate between since a student does not need to understand the word or hear the word clearly to select the correct word. The only task involved is listening for one syllable or more than one syllable. Sentences are given in the auditory training section under Q.I.E. rather than the homophenous words since use of the homophenous words would make the training too difficult for this step in the auditory training plan. Words are used in the auditory training section following Sentence Exercises to progress to a slightly more difficult step in training. At this step in the training plan, the student is required to understand the word rather than to listen for a word with one syllable contrasted with a two syllable word. Auditory training, following the Story Exercise, progresses to more difficult material where the student is required to differentiate between words that have minimal distinctive feature differences.

Chapter 3

PROCEDURE FOR ALL PLANS

I. **Quick Recognition Exercises:**
   A. *Write initial and final consonant Q.R.E. on the board.*
   B. *Use Total Communication to explain the meaning of the words.*
   C. *Point to the words in the first line and say them with a normally loud voic.*
   The student listens and watches (use amplification).
   Tactile cues may be provided if necessary.
   HE DOES NOT RESPOND AT THIS POINT.
   D. *Point to the words in the first line and say them with a normally loud voice.*
   Students say the words *with* the teacher.
   Order may be scrambled.
   The student listens and watches (use amplification).
   E. *Say the words in the first line with reduced loudness and without pointing.*
   Order may be scrambled.
   The student should rely on the vision for this step (use background music to control how much he hears).
   He says and/or signs the words in the order given.
   F. *Continue the above procedure for each of the lines of words. If students have good residual hearing, steps B, C, and D are eliminated.*

II. **Auditory Training:**
   Contrast words in the Q.R.E. with two words or multisyllabic words.
   A. *Write the words on the board.*
   B. *Point to the words in the first line and say them with a normally loud voice.*
   The student listens and watches (use amplification).

Tactile cues may be provided.
HE DOES NOT RESPOND AT THIS POINT.

C. *Have the student turn around. Say one of the words from the first line of words.*
Use amplification.
Student responds by saying and/or signing the word given.

D. *Continue the above procedure for each of the lines of words.*

III. **Quick Identification Exercises:**

A. *Ask the student to watch and try to speechread a Q.I.E. word.*
Say the word with reduced loudness.
Use background music to control how much he hears.
Do not write the word and/or sign the word.
Student responds by saying and/or signing the word given.
(He is correct if he responds with the word given or one of its homophenes.)

B. *Ask the student to close his eyes and imagine that you are saying the word again.*
Do not repeat the word at this point or write the word again or sign it.
Ask the student to tell other words that he thinks would be right.
Continue asking the student to think of words until all possible words are elicited.
May repeat the word at this step if there are remaining homophenes that have not been identified.

C. *Write the words on the board and make up sentences that clearly differentiate between the words.*
Use Total Communication to explain the meaning of the words and sign all sentences to ensure understanding.

D. *Point to the first sentence and say with a normally loud voice.*
The student listens and watches (use amplification).
Tactile cues may be provided.
HE DOES NOT RESPOND AT THIS POINT.

E. *Say either of the sentences with reduced loudness.*
Do not point to the sentence.
The student should rely on vision for this step (use background music to control how much he hears). He says and/or signs the sentence or he may identify the homophenous word used.

F. *Continue the above procedure with all sentences.*

IV. **Auditory Training:**
Use sentences given in Q.I.E.

A. *Write the sentences on the board and scramble the order.*

B. *Teacher holds a card in front of her face and says either of the sentences with a normally loud voice.*
Use amplification.
Student responds by saying and/or signing the sentence given.

C. *Continue the above procedure until all sentences are given.*

V. **Sentence Exercises with Clue Words:**
(Related or unrelated sentences may be used).

A. *Write the sentences and clue words on the board.*
Use Total Communication to explain the meaning of the words and sentences.

B. *Sign and say the clue word for the first sentence with a normally loud voice.*
The student listens and watches (use amplification).
Tactile cues may be provided if necessary.

C. *Say the first sentence with a normally loud voice.*
Do not sign the sentence.
The student listens and watches (use amplification).
Tactile cues may be provided if necessary.
He responds by saying and/or signing the sentence.

D. *Say the first sentence with reduced loudness.*
Do not sign the sentence.
The student should rely on vision for this step (use background music to control how much he hears).
Student responds by saying and/or signing the sentences.

E. *Scramble the order and continue the above procedure*

with all sentences.
VI. **Auditory Training:**
Use sentences given in Sentence Exercises with Clue Words.
  A. *Write the clue words given in the sentence exercises in scrambled order on the board.*
  B. *Have the student close his eyes. Say either of the clue words with a normally loud voice.*
  The student listens only (use amplification).
  Student responds by saying and/or signing the clue word given.
  C. *Continue the above procedure until all clue words are given.*
VII. **Story Exercises:**
  A. *Show a picture to clue the story.*
  Procedure for clueing the story may be varied by —
    1. Discussing a general topic from which the story is abstracted.
    2. Presenting a series of clue words.
    3. Presenting a series of clue sentences.
  B. *Use Total Communication to tell the story and to explain meaning.*
  Use a normally loud voice.
  Tactile cues may be provided.
  Student listens and watches (use amplification).
  C. *Tell the story with reduced loudness.*
  Student should rely on vision for this step (use background music to control how much he hears).
  Do not sign the story.
  D. *Students may vary their responses by repeating and/or signing each sentence or by answering questions about the story.*
VIII. **Auditory Training:**
Select words from the story that have minimal distinctive feature differences such as —

cage — cat

bears — bees

growl — grow

zoo — sew

swing — swim

Procedure:

A. *Write the words on the board.*
B. *Teacher holds a card in front of her face and says either of the words with a normally loud voice.*
   The student listens only (use amplification).
   The student responds by saying and/or signing the word given.
C. *Continue until all words are given.*

Chapter 4

PRESCHOOL LESSON PLANS

THE procedure for the preschool plans has been modified. Provision has been made at the beginning of each plan for the nursery rhyme to be told in simple form by using Total Communication. In Step I only initial consonant practice words are listed since final consonant practice words were found to be too difficult for preschool children. Q.I.E. training was eliminated, and auditory training with words with minimal distinctive feature differences was also eliminated. These steps also proved to be too difficult for preschool children. The procedure outlined in Chapter 3 should be followed for Steps II, III, IV, and V.

The following preschool plans are based on nursery rhymes from *The Real Mother Goose*, Rand McNally, 1974. It is felt that all children need exposure to the rhythm provided in them, and children usually love to listen to the rhymes even though they are not always understood. Due to the language difficulty it is suggested that dramatization and pictures be used with the presentation of all plans to aid in understanding.

Georgie Porgy Pudding and Pie   Jack Be Nimble
Hickory Dickory Dock   Little Miss Muffet
Humpty Dumpty   Mary Had A Little Lamb
Jack and Jill   This Little Piggy

GEORGY PORGY PUDDING AND PIE

Present the main idea of the rhyme in simple form:
Georgy Porgy is a boy.
He kisses the girls.
The girls cry.
The other boys come out to play.
Georgy Porgy runs.
  I. **Q.R.E.:**

INITIAL ONLY:

      pie   lie   sky

cry	fry	try
ran	fan	pan

II. **Auditory Training:**
    A. pie — pudding
    B. cry — playing
    C. ran — kissing

III. **Sentence Exercises:**

Georgy Porgy	A. Georgy Porgy kissed the girls.
kisses	B. The girls did not like the kisses.
play	C. Other boys came out to play.
ran away	D. Georgy Porgy ran away.
girls	E. Georgy Porgy likes to kiss girls.

IV. **Auditory Training:**
    A. kisses
    B. ran away
    C. girls
    D. play
    E. Georgy Porgy

V. **Story Exercises:**
    Present the nursery rhyme:
    Georgy Porgy Pudding and Pie
    Kissed the girls and made them cry;
    When the boys came out to play,
    Georgy Porgy ran away.
(*The Real Mother Goose*, Rand McNally, 1974)

HICKORY DICKORY DOCK

Present the main idea of the rhyme in simple form:
The mouse runs.
The mouse runs up the clock.
The clock is big and tall.
The clock says one o'clock.
It makes one "bong."
The mouse is scared.
The mouse runs down.

    I. **Q.R.E.:**

INITIAL ONLY:

one	fun	sun

clock	block	sock
ticks	picks	fix

II. **Auditory Training:**
A. one — ran up
B. clock — running
C. ticks — struck one

III. **Sentence Exercises:**
mouse   A. The mouse runs up the clock.
big   B. The clock is big and tall.
points   C. The little hand points to the one.
runs   D. The mouse runs down.
scared   E. The mouse is scared of the clock.

IV. **Auditory Training:**
A. scared
B. runs
C. big
D. mouse
E. points

V. **Story Exercises:**
Present the nursery rhyme:
Hickory, Dickory, Dock
The mouse ran up the clock.
The clock struck one,
The mouse ran down,
Hickory, Dickory, Dock.
(*The Real Mother Goose*, Rand NcNally, 1974)

HUMPTY DUMPTY

Present the main idea of the rhyme in simple form:
Humpty Dumpty sits on a wall.
He falls down.
He is an egg.
He breaks.
The king's horses and king's men cannot fix him.

I. **Q.R.E.**

INITIAL ONLY:

wall	fall	ball
sat	fat	bat

          men   thin   fin

II. **Auditory Training:**
   A. wall — Humpty Dumpty
   B. sat — horses
   C. men — fall down

III. **Sentence Exercises:**

Humpty Dumpty	A. Humpty Dumpty is an egg.
wall	B. He sits on a wall.
falls down	C. He falls down.
breaks	D. He breaks into lots of pieces.
fix	E. They cannot fix him.

IV. **Auditory Training:**
   A. falls down
   B. Humpty Dumpty
   C. breaks
   D. wall
   E. fix

V. **Story Exercises:**
   Present the nursery rhyme:
   Humpty Dumpty sat on the wall.
   Humpty Dumpty had a great fall.
   All the king's horses and all the king's men,
   Could not put Humpty Dumpty together again.
(*The Real Mother Goose*, Rand McNally, 1974)

JACK AND JILL

Present the main idea of the rhyme in simple form:
The girl and boy are walking.
They walk up the hill.
They want water.
They put the water in a bucket.
They fall down.
The girl and boy hurt their heads.

I. **Q.R.E.:**

INITIAL ONLY:

pail	fell	well
hill	pill	fill
broke	Coke®	woke

II. **Auditory Training:**

    A. pail — tumbling
    B. hill — fetching
    C. broke — fell down

III. **Sentence Exercises:**

girl and boy	A. A girl and boy walk up a hill.
water	B. They want a bucket of water.
hill	C. The water is on top of the hill.
fall down	D. The girl and boy fall down.
hurt	E. They hurt their heads.

IV. **Auditory Training:**
    A. hurt
    B. fall down
    C. hill
    D. water
    E. girl and boy

V. **Story Exercises:**
Present the nursery rhyme:
Jack and Jill went up the hill,
To fetch a pail of water.
Jack fell down and broke his crown,
And Jill came tumbling after.
(*The Real Mother Goose*, Rand McNally, 1974)

JACK BE NIMBLE

Present the main idea of the rhyme in simple form:
Jack jumps.
Jack jumps high and fast.
Jack jumps over the candle.
The candle is hot.
Jack does not want to get burned.

  I. **Q.R.E.:**

INITIAL ONLY:

fast	past	last
jump	bump	thumb
stick	pick	lick

II. **Auditory Training:**
    A. fast — nimble
    B. jump — burned
    C. stick — candle

III. **Sentence Exercises:**

jumps	A. Jack jumps high.
runs	B. Jack runs fast.
candle	C. The candle is on the floor.
over	D. Jack jumped over the candle.
fire	E. The fire is hot.

IV. **Auditory Training:**
   A. fire
   B. jumps
   C. runs
   D. candle
   E. over

V. **Story Exercises:**
   Present the nursery rhyme:
   Jack be nimble,
   Jack be quick,
   Jack jump over the candlestick.
(*The Real Mother Goose*, Rand McNally, 1974)

LITTLE MISS MUFFET

Present the main idea of the rhyme in simple form:
Miss Muffet sits.
Miss Muffet sits on a chair.
Miss Muffet eats.
Miss Muffet eats porridge.
A spider comes.
The spider scares Miss Muffet.
Miss Muffet runs away.

I. **Q.R.E.:**

INITIAL ONLY:

sat	fat	bat
fright	bite	kite
eat	feet	seat

II. **Auditory Training:**
   A. sat — spider
   B. fright — Miss Muffet
   C. eat — curds and whey

III. **Sentence Exercises:**

eats	A. Miss Muffet eats.
spider	B. A spider crawls up beside her.
jumps	C. Miss Muffet jumps and runs away.
spoon	D. The bowl and spoon fall down.
scared	E. Miss Muffet is scared of spiders.

IV. **Auditory Training:**
   A. spider
   B. scared
   C. spoon
   D. eats
   E. jumps

V. **Story Exercises:**
   Present the nursery rhyme:
   Little Miss Muffet sat on a tuffet,
   Eating of curds and whey.
   Along came a spider
   And sat down beside her.
   And frightened Miss Muffet away.
   (*The Real Mother Goose*, Rand McNally, 1974)

MARY HAD A LITTLE LAMB

Present the main idea of the rhyme in simple form:
Mary has a lamb.
The lamb is white.
The lamb likes Mary.
The lamb follows Mary to school.

I. **Q.R.E.:**

INITIAL ONLY:

had	bad	sad
snow	blow	go
went	bent	tent

II. **Auditory Training:**
   A. had — Mary
   B. snow — white wool
   C. went — little lamb

III. **Sentence Exercises:**

Mary	A. Mary has a pet lamb.
follows	B. The lamb follows Mary.

wool   C. The lamb has white wool.
school   D. The lamb goes to school with Mary.
laugh   E. The other children laugh.

IV. **Auditory Training:**
   A. school
   B. laugh
   C. wool
   D. Mary
   E. follows

V. **Story Exercises:**
Present the nursery rhyme:
Mary had a little lamb,
Its fleece was white as snow.
And everywhere that Mary went,
The lamb was sure to go.
(*The Real Mother Goose*, Rand McNally, 1974)

THIS LITTLE PIG (Five Toes)

Present the main idea of the rhyme in simple form:
One pig goes to the store.
One pig stays at home.
One pig eats meat.
One pig does not eat.
One pig cannot go home.

I. **Q.R.E.:**

INITIAL ONLY:

wee	tree	she
pig	lick	fig
stay	play	day

II. **Auditory Training:**
   A. home — roast beef
   B. pig — stay home
   C. stay — market

III. **Sentence Exercises:**
store   A. One pig goes to the store.
pig   B. There are five pigs.
home   C. I am going home.
crying   D. He is crying.

meat   E. I eat meat for lunch.

IV. **Auditory Training:**
   A. meat
   B. crying
   C. home
   D. pig
   E. store

V. **Story Exercises:**
   Present the nursery rhyme (use the fingers or toes to present this):
   This little pig went to market,
   This little pig stayed home;
   This little pig had roast beef,
   This little pig had none;
   This little pig said, "Wee, Wee;
   I can't find my way home."

(*The Real Mother Goose*, Rand McNally, 1974)

Chapter 5

LESSON PLANS FOR SCHOOL AGE CHILDREN

April Fool
Beach
Big Chicken
Birthday Party
Camping
Canoeing
Cat's Bath
Cat Chase
Circus
Dancing Class
Day At School
Don't Be a Litterbug
Easter Egg Hunt
Evil Mouse
Farm
Fish Tank
Friday Night Dance

Going to the Grocery Store
Halloween
Horses
Lions
Missing Pants
Mouse's Birthday Party
New Pet
Park
Playhouse
Pony
Snow
Swimming
Three Little Pigs
Tree House
Trip to the Library
Weather
Zoo

APRIL FOOL

I. **Q.R.E.:**

INITIAL:			FINAL:		
fool	pool	tool	mouth	mouse	mound
wish	fish	dish	lies	lime	live
face	pace	trace	nice	night	knife

II. **Auditory Training:**
   A. fool — good morning
   B. wish — tomorrow
   C. face — night light
   D. mouth — breakfast
   E. lies — woman
   F. nice — downstairs

III. **Q.I.E.:**
   Present the word *mask*.
   Possible correct responses are —
   mass
   pass
   bass
   mask   A. The woman put a mask on her face to

30

fool me.

mass	B. All good Catholics go to mass every Sunday.
pass	C. I hope to pass my exam tomorrow.
bass	D. We don't have bass to eat very often.

IV. **Auditory Training:**
   A. All good Catholics go to mass every Sunday.
   B. I hope I pass my exam tomorrow.
   C. The woman put a mask on her face to fool me.
   D. We don't have bass to eat very often.

V. **Sentence Exercises:**

fool	A. My mother fooled me on April Fool's Day.
face	B. My mother put a mask on her face to fool me.
wish	C. I wish I could tell when people are trying to fool me.
plate	D. Mother put a knife beside my plate at the table.

VI. **Auditory Training:**
   A. wish
   B. face
   C. fool
   D. plate

VII. **Story Exercises:**

I woke up this morning and put on my clothes. I went downstairs and walked into the kitchen to eat breakfast. I saw a strange woman setting the table. The woman said, "Good morning, you must be Tommy." The woman scared me because I didn't know who she was. I said, "Where is my mother?" The woman laughed and pulled off a mask. She said, "April Fool." Don't you think my mother was funny? I may try to fool my friends today at school.

VIII. **Auditory Training:**
   A. walked — talked
   B. laugh — bath
   C. she — me
   D. eat — feet
   E. clothes — bows

BEACH

I. **Q.R.E.:**

INITIAL:			FINAL:		
jaw	raw	paw	rough	rub	rush
wave	pave	save	shoes	shoot	shook
fin	thin	chin	beach	meat	beep

II. **Auditory Training:**
   A. jaw — shark teeth
   B. wave — sunburn
   C. fin — burned feet
   D. rough — swimming pool
   E. shoes — fishing pier
   F. beach — family

III. **Q.I.E.:**
   Present the word *sand*.
   Possible correct responses are —
   sat
   sad
   sand
   sat   A. The hot sand burned my feet.
   sad   B. I sat near the water and played.
           C. I am always sad when I leave the beach.

IV. **Auditory Training:**
   A. I sat near the water and played.
   B. I am always sad when I leave the beach.
   C. The hot sand burned my feet.

V. **Sentence Exercises:**
   beach   A. My family and I drove to the beach in four hours.
   waves   B. We could see the waves from our motel window.
   sunburn   C. I got a bad sunburn on my shoulder.
   fishing   D. My father and I went fishing on the pier.
   sailboat E. I saw a blue sailboat out in the ocean.

VI. **Auditory Training:**
   A. sunburn
   B. fishing
   C. waves
   D. beach
   E. sailboat

VII. **Story Exercises:**

My family and I went to the beach last June. I went swimming in the ocean and in the motel pool. The water was warm but the waves were rough. I played on a raft out in the ocean one day. I saw a shark fin near my raft. I thought it was "Jaws" ready to eat me. I swam to shore as fast as I could. I got out of the water and ran across the hot sand. My feet burned because I left my shoes on the beach. The shark fin was not "Jaws." It was only a piece of wood floating on top of the water.

I like to go to the beach with my family. We plan to go back to the beach next June.

VIII. **Auditory Training:**
    A. beach — beat
    B. shark — sharp
    C. sand — hand
    D. swim — fin
    E. float — boat

BIG CHICKEN

I. **Q.R.E.:**

INITIAL:			FINAL:		
egg	beg	leg	cook	cool	coop
feed	need	bead	chick	chip	chill
boy	toy	joy	bath	bad	bass

II. **Auditory Training:**
    A. egg — family
    B. feed — chickens
    C. boy — Billy
    D. cook — everyday
    E. chick — Saturday
    F. bath — popped

III. **Q.I.E.:**
Present the word *feed.*
Possible correct responses are —
feel
feet
feed   A. Billy went to the chicken house to feed the chickens.
feel   B. Snow makes you feel cold.

feet   C. My feet hurt when my shoes are too tight.

IV. **Auditory Training:**
   A. My feet hurt when my shoes are too tight.
   B. Billy went to the chicken house to feed the chickens.
   C. Snow makes you feel cold.

V. **Sentence Exercises:**
   chicken house A. Billy went to the chicken house to get some eggs.
   big egg   B. He picked up a very big egg.
   chicken   C. A big white chicken popped out.
   walk   D. He took the big chicken for a walk.
   pet   E. Billy has a new pet chicken.

VI. **Auditory Training:**
   A. pet
   B. chicken
   C. big egg
   D. walk
   E. chicken house

VII. **Story Exercises:**
Billy got up early last Saturday. He put on his coat and walked to the chicken house. He went to the chicken house to get some eggs and feed the chickens. Billy picked up a very big egg. A big white chicken popped out of the big egg. Billy was surprised to see such a big chicken. He tried to carry the chicken to his house. He could not pick up the big chicken. He took the chicken for a walk. Billy said, "I'll keep this big chicken for a pet." He and the big chicken go for a walk every day. They always have fun.

VIII. **Auditory Training:**
   A. feed — feet
   B. coat — goat
   C. his — is
   D. tried — lied
   E. big — bet

BIRTHDAY PARTY

I. Q.R.E.:

INITIAL:			FINAL:		
cake	bake	take	room	roof	rule
sing	ring	king	ate	ache	aim
game	same	name	bus	bud	bunch

II. Auditory Training:
A. cake — birthday party   D. room — mountain
B. sing — presents   E. ate — candles
C. game — chocolate cake   F. bus — everybody

III. Q.I.E.:
Present the word *punch.*
Possible correct responses are —
bunch
munch
punch   A. We drank punch at the birthday party.
bunch   B. I picked a bunch of flowers.
munch   C. Potato chips are good to munch.
Present the word *pies.*
Possible correct responses are —
buys
mice
pies   A. Mother baked some pies for my birthday party.
buys   B. Daddy buys me some candy every day.
mice   C. We sang "Three Blind Mice" at my birthday
        party.

IV. Auditory Training:
A. I picked a bunch of flowers.
B. We drank punch at the birthday party.
C. Potato chips are good to munch.
D. We sang "Three Blind Mice" at my birthday party.
E. Mother baked some pies for my birthday party.
F. Daddy buys me some candy everyday.

V. Sentence Exercises:
presents   A. My friends brought me some birthday
            presents today.
balloons   B. We blew up balloons for the party.
ribbons   C. There were many pretty ribbons on
            the package.

   birthday   D. I turned five on this birthday.
   play   E. I want to play with my new presents.

VI. **Auditory Training:**
   A. play
   B. ribbons
   C. presents
   D. balloons
   E. birthday

VII. **Story Exercises:**

Mom gave me a party on my birthday. She baked a chocolate cake and bought some candy. My friends came over for the party. Mom put the cake and candy on the dining room table. One of my friends said, "I want to sing 'Happy Birthday' to you." Everybody sang "Happy Birthday," and I blew out the candles. Mom gave us some punch to drink, and we all ate a bunch of cake and candy.

We played some games. We played "King of the Mountain," "Ring around the Rosie," and "Pin the Tail on the Donkey." Everybody liked to play "Pin the Tail on the Donkey." We played that game three times. We thought of a new name for "Pin the Tail on the Donkey." It should be called "The Donkey's Sore Body." Everybody had a good time at my birthday party.

VIII. **Auditory Training:**
   A. fame — same
   B. play — day
   C. bake — cake
   D. table — label
   E. blew — to

CAMPING

I. **Q.R.E.:**

Initial:			Final:		
sun	run	bun	rose	rope	rove
food	mood	hood	rat	rash	rag
bug	rug	tug	camp	calf	cat

II. **Auditory Training:**
   A. sun — fishing pole
   B. food — sunshine

    C. bug — Indian chief

    D. rose — sleeping bag

    E. rat — bunk bed

    F. camp — outhouse

III. **Q.I.E.:**

Present the word *bed*.

Possible correct responses are —

bell

belt

met

men

pet

bed   A. My bed at camp was very warm.

bell   B. The bell went off when we had to go to sleep.

belt   C. I made an Indian belt out of leather.

met   D. I met a real live Indian chief at the campfire.

men   E. The men at camp were strong and big.

pet   F. We couldn't take pets to camp with us.

IV. **Auditory Training:**

    A. The men at camp were strong and big.

    B. My bed at camp was very warm.

    C. I made an Indian belt out of leather.

    D. We couldn't take pets to camp with us.

    E. The bell went off when we had to go to sleep.

    F. I met a real live Indian chief at the camp.

V. **Sentence Exercises:**

camp   A. I went to camp in the woods.

duck   B. We fed the duck in the pond.

food   C. The food at camp tasted bad.

bathroom D. We used outhouses for bathrooms at camp.

bugs   E. Bugs crawled around us all of the time.

brushed   F. I brushed the bugs away with my hand.

VI. **Auditory Training:**

    A. bugs

    B. food

    C. duck

    D. camp

E. brushed

F. bathroom

VII. **Story Exercises:**

I went to camp last summer. The camp was far away from my house. It was in the woods beside a pond. The camp had a cabin made out of logs. I slept in a cabin with bunk beds. The beds were soft and warm. There were six boys in each cabin. A man lived with us. He was called the counselor. He made us keep the cabin clean.

We went fishing in the pond. I caught three fish. We made a camp fire every night at the pond. An Indian chief came and sat with us at the camp fire one night. I loved my cabin in the woods. I want to go again next summer.

VIII. **Auditory Training:**

A. pond — pan

B. house — mouse

C. fish — dish

D. chief — cheat

E. wood — food

CANOEING

I. **Q.R.E.:**

INITIAL:			FINAL:		
stuck	duck	truck	went	whip	wish
dad	mad	sad	safe	sale	same
mom	Tom	from	home	hole	hose

II. **Auditory Training:**

A. stuck — canoeing

B. dad — unstuck

C. mom — paddling

D. went — happened

E. safe — getting

F. home — safely

III. **Q.I.E.:**

Present the word *stuck*.

Possible correct responses are —

stick

slick

stuck   A. The canoe got stuck in the sand.

 stick B. The boy threw a stick into the water.

 slick C. The little girl fell on the slick ice and hurt her head.

IV. **Auditory Training:**
 A. The boy threw a stick into the water.
 B. The little girl fell on the slick ice and hurt her head.
 C. The canoe got stuck in the sand.

V. **Sentence Exercises:**

 canoeing A. Two boys went canoeing.

 rough water B. They ran into rough water.

 jumped out C. They jumped out of the canoe and swam to shore.

 home D. The boys ran home to tell their parents.

 scared E. They don't want to go canoeing again.

VI. **Auditory Training:**
 A. canoeing
 B. rough water
 C. scared
 D. jumped out
 E. home

VII. **Story Exercises:**

Two little boys wanted to go canoeing. One boy's name was Tom, and the other boy's name was John. Tom asked his mother if he could go to the river. His mother said, "Yes, but be careful and don't go near the part of the river where there is a waterfall." John asked his dad and his dad said, "Yes, but you must wear a life jacket." They got up early on Saturday morning and headed for the river. They had trouble getting the canoe into the water. It got stuck in the sand. They finally got it unstuck and into the water. Tom and John were on their way down the river finally. They enjoyed paddling very much and started to go very fast. They came to the part of the river where the water was fast before they knew it. They heard a loud roar. Tom and John got scared and jumped out of the canoe. They swam to land just in time to see the canoe go over the waterfall. They ran home and told their parents what happened. They didn't go back to that part of the river again.

VIII. **Auditory Training:**
A. trouble — double
B. fast — passed
C. stuck — stick
D. sand — send

CAT'S BATH

I. **Q.R.E.:**

Initial:			Final:		
tree	free	three	branch	break	brand
tub	rub	scrub	ran	rag	raise
come	some	hum	reach	real	rake

II. **Auditory Training:**
A. tree — decided
B. tub — children
C. come — climbed
D. branch — ladder
E. ran — wouldn't
F. reach — favorite

III. **Q.I.E.:**
Present the word *food*.
Possible correct responses are —
foot
fool
food A. The little girl gave her cat some food.
foot B. The tall boy hurt his foot on a piece of glass.
fool C. Are you trying to fool me?

IV. **Auditory Training:**
A. Are you trying to fool me?
B. The tall boy hurt his foot on a piece of glass.
C. The little girl gave her cat some food.

V. **Sentence Exercises:**

dirty	A. The little girl's cat needs a bath.
bath	B. The cat doesn't like water.
scared	C. He ran away and climbed a tree.
cat	D. The cat wouldn't come down out of the tree.
help	E. Daddy brought a ladder and got the cat down.

safe   F. The little girl was happy to have her
                          cat back.
VI. **Auditory Training:**
   A. bath
   B. cat
   C. dirty
   D. help
   E. safe
   F. scared
VII. **Story Exercises:**
   The little girl decided to give her cat a bath. The cat was very
dirty. She filled the bath tub with water. Her brother helped.
The cat didn't like the water. He was scared. The cat ran away
from the girl and boy. He ran to a tree and climbed up. The cat
climbed on a branch. The children tried to get the cat to come
down. The cat wouldn't come down to eat his favorite food.
The girl and boy called their daddy for help. He brought a
ladder so he could reach the cat. He brought the cat down from
the tree. The children were very happy to have their cat
back.
VIII. **Auditory Training:**
   A. cat — cut   D. boy — toy
   B. food — foot   E. tub — thumb
   C. branch — prank

CAT CHASE

I. **Q.R.E.:**

INITIAL:			FINAL:		
cat	sat	fat	log	lot	loss
ship	whip	flip	mad	match	map
pet	get	let	catch	cap	cat

II. **Auditory Training:**
   A. cat — cabin
   B. ship — jumped
   C. pet — captain
   D. log — good-bye
   E. mad — decided
   F. catch — finally
III. **Q.I.E.:**

Present the word *cat*.
Possible correct responses —
can
call
cat   A. The boy tried to catch the cat.
can B. Will you open a can of soup for me?
call C. Please call me when you get back to school.

IV. **Auditory Training:**
    A. Please call me when you get back to school.
    B. Will you open a can of soup for me?
    C. The boy tried to catch the cat.

V. **Sentence Exercises:**

cat	A. A little boy saw a cat and tried to catch it.
ran away	B. The cat ran away from the boy.
hid	C. The cat hid in an old crate.
fell	D. The little boy climbed on top of the crate and fell in on top of the cat.
caught	E. The captain caught the cat.
gave	F. The captain gave the cat to the little boy.

VI. **Auditory Training:**
    A. fell
    B. ran away
    C. hid
    D. caught
    E. gave
    F. cat

VII. **Story Exercises:**

A little boy named John saw a cat and decided to catch it. The cat ran away and he chased it. He almost got hit by a car while he was trying to catch the cat. He kept running after it. The cat ran to a loading dock and hid in a crate. John climbed up on the crates to catch the cat. He looked inside one crate and there was the cat. He fell inside the crate right on top of the cat. He scared the cat, but he caught it. The boy felt the crate move and looked out. A man was picking the crate up in the air. He put the crate on a ship. The boy climbed up to the deck from the bottom of the ship. He looked out, and the captain caught him. The captain said, "What are you doing on my ship?" John said, "I am chasing a cat." The captain got mad at John and took him to a cabin and told him to stay there. The captain went to his cabin to write in his log book.

The cat ran into the captain's cabin. He jumped up on his desk and spilled ink all over the log book. The captain got mad and chased the cat. He caught the cat by the tail. He was about to throw the cat off the ship, but John said, "No don't do it." Finally, the captain said, "All right," and gave the cat back to John. The captain put John and the cat on a small boat and sent them back to shore. They waved good-bye to the captain and went home. The boy was glad to have a cat at last.

VIII. **Auditory Training:**
   A. saw — sew
   B. fell — feel
   C. log — fog
   D. tail — tape
   E. ship — sheep
   F. kept — keep

CIRCUS

I. **Q.R.E.:**

INITIAL:			FINAL:		
hat	pat	fat	cage	cape	cave
clown	frown	brown	dog	not	top
bear	hair	wear	peg	pet	best

II. **Auditory Training:**
   A. hat — lion tamer   E. dog — center
   B. clown — elephant   F. peg — funny
   C. bear — circus ring
   D. cage — ballons

III. **Q.I.E.:**
   Present the word *band*.
   Possible correct responses are —
   man
   mad
   pat

band   A. The band played good music at the circus.
man   B. The shortest man on earth ran around
                  the center ring.
mad   C. The lion tamer got mad at one of the lions.
pat   D. I wanted to pat the seal, but I was afraid.
  IV. **Auditory Training:**
       A. The shortest man on earth ran around the center ring.
       B. I wanted to pat the seal, but I was afraid.
       C. The band played good music at the circus.
       D. The lion tamer got mad at one of the lions.
   V. **Sentence Exercises:**
       clowns   A. The clowns made me laugh.
       animals   B. I saw many animals at the circus.
       shortest   C. I saw the shortest man on earth at the
                          circus.
       lions   D. The lions roared at the lion tamer.
       circus   E. The circus comes to our town every
                          fall.
  VI. **Auditory Training:**
       A. animals
       B. shortest
       C. circus
       D. clowns
       E. lions
 VII. **Story Exercises:**
   I went to the circus at the coliseum last fall. Daddy stood in a
long line to buy our tickets. We sat behind the band, and it was
very loud. The clowns came out first. I saw a fat clown with a
dog. He had a sad face. A tall man with a big hat came out
next. He was very funny. The shortest man on earth popped
out of a little box. The shortest man on earth chased the tallest
man around the ring. I laughed and laughed.
   The animals came out to the center ring after the clowns left.
There were lions, tigers, elephants, and horses. The lions and
tigers were in big cages. A man with a whip made them do
funny tricks. I liked the elephants best. The circus was fun. I
want to go again next fall.
VIII. **Auditory Training:**
       A. trick — truck
       B. ring — sing

C. hat — pat
D. big — wig
E. popped — mopped
F. tap — nap
G. lap — lamb
H. sad — had

DANCING CLASS

I. **Q.R.E.:**

INITIAL:			FINAL:		
went	sent	lent	tap	tan	tang
day	hay	may	red	rest	wreck
tap	map	wrap			
sing	ring	king			

II. **Auditory Training:**
   A. went — dance recital
   B. day — costume
   C. tap — dancing shoes
   D. sing — auditorium
   E. red — music plays

III. **Q.I.E.:**
   Present the word *tap*.
   Possible correct responses are —
   nap
   lap
   lamb

   tap   A. I am learning to tap dance on Thursdays.

   nap   B. I don't have to take a nap on the day that I have dance class.

   lap   C. I sleep with a teddy bear on my lap.

   lamb   D. Mary had a little lamb.

IV. **Auditory Training:**
   A. I sleep with a teddy bear on my lap.
   B. I am learning to tap dance on Thursdays.
   C. Mary had a little lamb.
   D. I don't have to take a nap on the day that I have dance class.

V. **Sentence Exercises:**

dance	A. I went to dance class last Thursday.
sing	B. We sing and dance in our class.
favorite	C. Tap is my favorite dance.
pants	D. I wear red pants to my dance class.
recital	E. I will tap dance at the recital.

VI. **Auditory Training:**
 A. recital
 B. favorite
 C. sing
 D. dance
 E. pants

VII. **Story Exercises:**

I went to tap dance class last Thursday. We danced for two hours. I got very tired. The teacher said we will get new red dresses for our recital in May. My parents will come to the recital. I will dance and sing while the teacher plays a record. I can't wait for the recital. I hope you can come to see me dance.

VIII. **Auditory Training:**
 A. dance — pants
 B. drew — press
 C. plays — days
 D. tired — fixed
 E. wait — make

DAY AT SCHOOL

I. **Q.R.E.:**

INITIAL:			FINAL:		
day	they	say	like	life	line
lunch	bunch	crunch	job	John	jog
			dash	day	dad

II. **Auditory Training:**
 A. day — afternoon   C. like — study
 B. lunch — spaghetti   D. job — teacher
     E. dash — practice

III. **Q.I.E.:**
Present the word *yard*.
Possible correct responses are —

yarn
art
hard
heart

yard	A. We run in the school yard every day.
yarn	B. We made a ball out of yarn.
art	C. I love to go to art class once a week.
hard	D. All of my subjects are very hard for me.
heart	E. We are studying about the heart in health class.

IV. **Auditory Training:**
   A. We made a ball out of yarn.
   B. All of my subjects are very hard for me.
   C. We run in the school yard every day.
   D. We are studying about the heart in health class.
   E. I love to go to art class once a week.

V. **Sentence Exercises:**

reading	A. We are going to reading class today.
job	B. I have to clean the art center after school.
puppet	C. I will show you how to make a puppet in study hall.
vacuum	D. I like to sweep the floor and vacuum the rug.

VI. **Auditory Training:**
   A. vacuum
   B. job
   C. puppet
   D. reading

VII. **Story Exercises:**

My friends and I have many things to do during the day. We go to reading in the morning. We go to P.E. and art class in the afternoon. We run in the school yard during P.E. class and at lunch time. In P.E. class we are practicing for field day. I'll run the forty yard dash. I plan to cross the finish line first. We are making puppets in art class. I am making a puppet that looks like a dog. He has a big red mouth and blue eyes. After class there is always a mess on the floor. I always vacuum the rug after class and pick up all of my materials. The fun part of the day is when we line up to catch the bus for home.

VIII. **Auditory Training:**
A. class — pass   D. floor — more
B. mouth — mouse   E. yard — card
C. read — feed

DON'T BE A LITTERBUG

I. **Q.R.E.:**

INITIAL:			FINAL:		
boy	toy	joy	bench	bed	best
park	dark	shark	pick	pin	miss
money	funny	honey	stick	step	still

II. **Auditory Training:**
A. boy — ice cream
B. park — seventy-five cents
C. money — walking
D. bench — fudgesicle
E. pick — around
F. stick — pick up

III. **Q.I.E.:**
Present the word *money.*
Possible correct responses are —
bunny
muddy
buddy

money   A. Do you have enough money to buy ice cream?
bunny   B. The bunny bit the little boy's finger.
muddy   C. Your shoes are muddy.
buddy   D. I have a new buddy at school.

IV. **Auditory Training:**
A. Your shoes are muddy.
B. The bunny bit the little boy's finger.
C. I have a new buddy at school.
D. Do you have enough money to buy ice cream?

V. **Sentence Exercises:**
trash   A. Will you clean up the trash around

	the yard?
cleaned up	B. Tom cleaned up all the trash around the yard.
seventy-five cents	C. His mother gave him seventy-five cents.
ice cream	D. Tom bought some ice cream.
park	E. He took a walk in the park and ate the ice cream.
trash	F. He saw a lot of trash in the park.

VI. **Auditory Training:**
   A. cleaned up
   B. ice cream
   C. park
   D. trash
   E. seventy-five cents

VII. **Story Exercises:**

One day Tom's mother said, "Tom will you help clean up the trash around the yard?" Tom picked up all the trash and put it in the garbage can. His mother gave him seventy-five cents. He went to the store and bought some ice cream. He bought a fudgesicle. The man at the store said, "That will be fifty-five cents," and handed him the ice cream. Tom walked to the park and ate his ice cream. He saw a lot of trash in the park. He thought, I'd hate to pick up all this trash.

When Tom saw a trash can he thought about his ice cream stick. He thought, this is trash, too. I'll throw my stick in the trash can.

VIII. **Auditory Training:**
   A. pick — stick
   B. teeth — death
   C. cream — steam
   D. trash — crash
   E. yard — hard
   F. pick — peck

EASTER EGG HUNT

I. **Q.R.E.:**

INITAL:			FINAL:		
egg	beg	leg	best	beg	Beth
dye	buy	fly	live	light	like
best	nest	guess	bush	bug	bull

II. **Auditory Training:**
   A. egg — bunny
   B. dye — chicken
   C. best — Easter
   D. best — candy
   E. live — animal
   F. bush — chocolate

III. **Q.I.E.:**
   Present the word *park*.
   Possible correct responses are —
   bark
   mark
   park   A. I am going to the park.
   bark   B. The dog will bark at people.
   mark   C. I put a mark on my pants.

IV. **Auditory Training:**
   A. I put a mark on my pants.
   B. The dog will bark at people.
   C. I am going to the park.

V. **Sentence Exercises:**
   paints   A. My mother paints the eggs at Easter.
   help   B. I like to help my mother.
   basket   C. I have an Easter basket.
   hunt   D. We went to the Easter egg hunt.
   chicken   E. I want a real live chicken.

VI. **Auditory Training:**
   A. help
   B. paints
   C. hunt
   D. chicken
   E. basket

VII. **Story Exercises:**
   We went to the Easter egg hunt. I found three eggs. My sister

found eight. My sister is older than me. We looked for eggs in the park. They put some eggs under the bushes. Some of the Easter eggs are chocolate. They put toys in the plastic eggs. I am waiting for the Easter bunny.

VIII. **Auditory Training:**
  A. park — bark
  B. eggs — begs
  C. me — meat
  D. some — sun
  E. bunny — honey

EVIL MOUSE

I. **Q.R.E.:**

INITIAL:			FINAL:		
hill	will	pill	mice	bite	pipe
green	bean	seed	mean	peas	beef
stick	pig	fig	room	root	roof
ride	slide	fight			

II. **Auditory Training:**
  A. hill — castle
  B. green — mean mouse
  C. stick — window
  D. ride — skipped
  E. mice — jumped
  F. mean — dragon
  G. room — followed

III. **Q.I.E.:**
Present the word *mad*.
Possible correct responses are —
pad
ball
bat
pal

mad	A. The mouse was very mad at the mice.
pad	B. A frog likes to sit on a lily pad.
ball	C. I play ball with my friends in the park.
bat	D. The bat flew out of the cave and scared the boy.

pal   E. My pal's name is Billy.
IV. Auditory Training:
A. A frog likes to sit on a lily pad.
B. I play ball with my friends in the park.
C. My pal's name is Billy.
D. The mouse was very mad at the mice.
E. The bat flew out of the cave and scared the boy.

V. Sentence Exercises:

locked in   A. An evil mouse locked the prince and princess in a deserted castle.

scared   B. They were frightened by bats and a dragon.

escaped   C. The prince and princess climbed out of a window.

helped   D. A friendly frog gave them a ride on a lily pad.

revenge   E. The prince and princess knocked the evil mouse into the water.

VI. Auditory Training:
A. scared
B. escaped
C. locked in
D. revenge
E. helped

VII. Story Exercises:

An evil mouse locked the prince and princess mice in a deserted castle. They were frightened by bats flying around and by a big green dragon. The mouse prince protected the princess from the bats and dragon. They escaped by climbing out a window and jumping into the moat. A friendly frog gave them a ride to the shore on his lily pad. They were happy to be safe. They saw the evil mouse on their way home. They were very quiet as they got behind the evil mouse. The prince hit the evil mouse with his stick. The mouse fell head first into the water. He was very, very mad at the two mice. The prince and princess were very happy. They skipped and jumped and laughed all the way home. They were happy to get home again and sit in front of the fire.*

---

*Goodall, John S.: *Creepy Castles*, New York, Atheneum Pub. Co., 1975.

VIII. **Auditory Training:**
   A. prince — princess
   B. mad — pad
   C. hit — heat
   D. bats — bets
   E. skip — ship

FARM

I. **Q.R.E.:**

INITIAL:			FINAL:		
barn	yard	lard	calf	cab	cat
sheep	reap	peep	sleep	sleeve	sleet
pig	fig	wig	lamb	laugh	land

II. **Auditory Training:**
   A. barn — feeding
   B. sheep — rooster
   C. pig — barnyard
   D. calf — moo cow
   E. sleep — tomatoes
   F. lamb — animals

III. **Q.I.E.:**
Present the word *pig.*
Possible correct responses are —
big
pick
beak
peek

pig   A. The pig eats slop and rolls in the mud.
big   B. The farm is very big.
pick   C. I picked six tomatoes this morning.
beak   D. The duck's beak is broken.
peek   E. I will peek in to see if the hen is laying an egg.

IV. **Auditory Training:**
   A. I will peek in to see if the hen is laying an egg.
   B. The pig eats slop and rolls in the mud.
   C. The farm is very big.
   D. The duck's beak is broken.

E. I picked six tomatoes this morning.

V. **Sentence Exercises:**

baby	A. The baby cow is called a calf.
pig	B. The fat pig is muddy.
feed	C. We feed the pigs and cows every morning.
rooster	D. The rooster wakes us up every morning.
work	E. The farmer works in the field all day.

VI. **Auditory Training:**
   A. pig
   B. baby
   C. work
   D. rooster
   E. feed

VII. **Story Exercises:**

Penny lives on a farm. There are many animals on her farm. Penny's favorite animal is a pig named Fatty. Fatty plays in the mud. Penny feeds Fatty and the other animals every morning. The rooster crows when the sun comes up. The rooster wakes Penny up, and she feeds the animals. Penny likes to live on a farm. Would you like to live on a farm?

VIII. **Auditory Training:**

   A. mud — bud   D. live — give
   B. farm — charm   E. play — way
   C. sun — fun

FISH TANK

I. **Q.R.E.:**

INITIAL:			FINAL:		
fish	wish	dish	bit	big	bib
boy	toy	joy	fish	fit	fir
tank	sank	bank	ate	ape	age
blow	flow	slow			

II. **Auditory Training:**
   A. fish — zebra
   B. boy — temperature

C. tank — homework
D. blow — cold water
E. bit — Mother
F. ate — blowfish

III. **Q.I.E.:**
Present the word *fed*.
Possible correct responses are —
fell
fin
fill

fed	A. Billy fed his fish everyday.
fell	B. The little boy fell down and hurt his knee.
fin	C. Fish have fins to help them swim.
fill	D. Billy had to fill the tank with water.

IV. **Auditory Training**
   A. Billy had to fill the tank with water.
   B. Fish have fins to help them swim.
   C. The little boy fell down and hurt his knee.
   D. Billy fed his fish everyday.

V. **Sentence Exercises:**

fish	A. Billy had seven fish in his tank.
cold water	B. Fish don't like cold water in the tank.
blowfish	C. He had some blowfish in his tank.
fed	D. Billy fed his fish everyday.

VI. **Auditory Training**
   A. cold water
   B. fed
   C. blowfish
   D. fish

VII. **Story Exercises:**
Billy saved his money and bought a fish tank. He bought six fish, and his mother gave him seven more fish. Billy filled the new tank with warm water. Fish don't like to swim in cold water. He put all of the fish in the tank and watched them swim. He counted six bluefish and five blowfish. He had two zebra fish.
Billy fed his fish every day, but they only ate a little food. He

always did his homework near the tank. He liked to watch the fish swim. How many fish did Billy have?

VIII. **Auditory Training:**
    A. fish — feet
    B. blow — blue
    C. cold — hold
    D. fed — feed

FRIDAY NIGHT DANCE

I. **Q.R.E.:**

INITIAL:			FINAL:		
dance	pants	chance	band	back	bath
night	might	fight	play	plate	place
band	hand	fanned	beach	beat	bees

II. **Auditory Training:**
    A. dance — music
    B. night — rock 'n roll
    C. band — practice
    D. play — dating
    E. beach — disco

III. **Q.I.E.:**

Present the word *band*.

Possible correct responses are —
bail
bat
bad
pan
pail

band   A. The band played until one o'clock.
bail   B. I will put up the bail.
bat   C. The bat is broken.
bad   D. I am a bad dancer.
pan   E. Cook my eggs in the frying pan.
pail   F. We put out a pail to catch the drip.

Present the word *man*.

Possible correct responses are —
mail
male

mat
mad
man   G. The man at the door checked I.D.s.
mail   H. My invitation arrived in the mail.
male   I. The band members are all male.
mat   J. We put a mat down to dance on.
mad   K. I am mad about the party ending at
             one o'clock.

IV. **Auditory Training:**
   A. I am mad about the party ending at one o'clock.
   B. I put up the bail.
   C. The bat is broken.
   D. We put out a pail to catch the drip.
   E. The man at the door checked I.D.s.
   F. The band members are all male.
   G. The band played until one o'clock.
   H. I am a bad dancer.
   I. We put a mat down to dance on.
   J. My invitation arrived by mail.
   K. Cook my eggs in the frying pan.

V. **Sentence Exercises:**
   high school   A. Our high school has a winter dance
                   every year.
   music   B. We like all kinds of music.
   beat   C. I cannot keep the beat very well.
   bass   D. I really like the bass most of all.
   band   E. The band that is playing is from
                   Washington, D.C.

Auditory Training:
   A. music
   B. band
   C. high school
   D. beat
   E. bass

VII. **Story Exercises:**
   We are going to the high school dance Friday night. I have a date, and I borrowed the car from my dad. The band that is playing is very good. They play rock and roll and beach music. My date knows how to disco dance. She is in a dance club. I am

going with her to the club Wednesday night. We are going to practice together. I hope I can learn how to dance.

VIII. **Auditory Training:**
    A. date — late
    B. play — day
    C. drum — hum
    D. dance — plans
    E. club — rub

GOING TO THE GROCERY STORE

I. **Q.R.E.:**

INITIAL:			FINAL:		
store	floor	more	ball	bath	bag
cart	heart	start	pack	path	pass
buys	flies	tries	cake	came	care
grill	fill	hill			

II. **Auditory Training:**
    A. store — hungry
    B. cart — dinner
    C. buys — hamburgers
    D. grill — cookouts
    E. ball — grocery
    F. pack — lettuce
    G. cake — cereal

III. **Q.I.E.:**
Present the word *buy*.
Possible correct responses are —
pie
my

buy	A. Will you buy some milk at the store?
pie	B. I'll have another piece of pie, please.
my	C. My book is the one with the torn page.

IV. **Auditory Training:**
    A. I'll have another piece of pie, please.
    B. Will you buy some milk at the store?
    C. My book is the one with the torn page.

V. **Sentence Exercises:**

PRIMARY:

grocery store A. My mother goes to the grocery store every week.

shopping cart B. I push the shopping cart when I go with her.

money C. Mom gives the lady some money.

helps D. The man helps put the bags in our car.

dinner E. She bought noodles and peas for dinner last week.

ELEMENTARY:

cookout A. We want to have a cookout.

grocery store B. Mother needs to go to the grocery store to buy the food.

chef C. Dad will be the chef because he likes to cook on the grill.

relax D. We always relax at family cookouts.

hungry E. We all get very hungry.

VI. Auditory Training:

PRIMARY:	ELEMENTARY:
A. money	A. grocery store
B. dinner	B. chef
C. helps	C. cookout
D. shopping cart	D. hungry
E. grocery store	E. relax

VII. Story Exercises:

PRIMARY:

My mother has to go to the grocery store every week. She comes home with many boxes and bags of food. She buys meat and fish. I push the shopping cart if I go with her. She bought noodles and peas for dinner last week. I like to go with her. I pick out nuts and cake and bubble gum. Mom gives the lady some money. The man helps put the bags in our car.

ELEMENTARY:

We want to have a cookout. Mother needs to go to the grocery store to buy the food. She will buy hamburgers, hot dogs, and mustard. We need paper plates, napkins, buns, and a pack of chips. I want lettuce and Fritos® too. Dad will be the chef because he likes to cook on the grill. We always relax at family cookouts. Everyone like to play ball or frisbee before dinner. We all get very hungry, though. I wish we had cookouts every week.

VIII. **Auditory Training:**

PRIMARY:	ELEMENTARY:
A. bags — begs	A. buy — my
B. gum — gun	B. chips — ships
C. fish — feet	C. bubble — double
D. peas — bees	D. grill — gill

HALLOWEEN

I. **Q.R.E:**

INITIAL:			FINAL:		
mask	task	ask	mask	map	mad
scare	tear	bear	witch	whip	win
ghost	most	toast	trick	trip	trend

II. **Auditory Training:**
   A. mask — Halloween
   B. scare — trick or treat
   C. ghost — afraid
   D. witch — broom stick
   E. trick — full moon

III. **Q.I.E.:**
   Present the word *witch*.
   Possible correct responses are —
   win
   will

   witch   A. The witch rides on a broom.
   win   B. I can win the costume contest.
   will   C. I will make a scary mask.

IV. **Auditory Training:**
   A. I will make a scary mask.
   B. The witch rides on a broom.
   C. I can win the costume contest.

V. **Sentence Exercises:**
   Halloween   A. The trick or treaters come on Halloween.
   moon   b. The moon is full and bright.

candy	C. I carry a bag for my candy.
costume	D. My costume is very scary.
mask	E. We made Halloween masks at school.

VI. **Auditory Training:**
   A. costume
   B. Halloween
   C. moon
   D. mask
   E. candy

VII. **Story Exercises:**
The witch is stirring the pot. The owl is sitting in the tree. He is watching the witch. Another witch flew up on a broom. She helped the first witch. They finished the brew and drank it. There was fire and smoke. When it went away the witches were gone. The only thing left was a broom in a puddle of water. The wise owl knew it must be Halloween.

VIII. **Auditory Training:**
   A. pot — hot
   B. watch — ship
   C. treat — trick
   D. mask — map
   E. ghost — most

HORSES

I. **Q.R.E.:**

INITIAL:			FINAL:		
trash	mash	crash	told	toes	took
red	bed	said	best	beg	bed
stable	table	able	wash	walk	wall
book	took	hook			

II. **Auditory Training:**
   A. trash — library
   B. red — surprise
   C. stable — opened
   D. book — birthday
   E. told — daddy
   F. best — horses
   G. wash — helped

III. **Q.I.E.:**
Present the word *horse*.
Possible correct responses are —
house
| *horse* | A. The big red horse is in the stable. |
| *house* | B. Beth lives in a white house with her mother and daddy. |

IV. **Auditory Training:**
  A. Beth lives in a white house with her mother and daddy.
  B. The big red horse is in the stable.

V. **Sentence Exercises:**
book	A. Beth went to the library to find a book about horses.
horse	B. She wants a horse for her birthday.
wash dishes	C. She helps her mother wash dishes everyday.
rake	D. She helps her daddy rake the yard.
surprise	E. She got a good suprise for her birthday.

VI. **Auditory Training:**
  A. wash dishes
  B. rake
  C. book
  D. horse
  E. surprise

VII. **Story Exercises:**
Beth went to the library to find a book. The librarian said, "What kind of book do you want?" Beth said, "I love horses, so I want a book about horses." She took the book home and told her mother that she wanted a horse for her birthday. Her mother said, "You might get a horse if you help with the chores around the house." Beth worked very hard every day. She helped her mother wash dishes and carried out the trash. She raked the yard for her daddy and helped him wash the car. When her birthday came her daddy said, "Come with me and see your surprise." They went to the stable and opened the door. Beth saw the prettiest red horse in the world. She said, "This is the best birthday present I ever had." She ran over to

her new horse and kissed him.
VIII. **Auditory Training:**
    A. Beth — bath C. took — look E. horse — house
    B. read — red D. yard — hard

LIONS

I. **Q.R.E.:**

INITIAL:			FINAL:		
paw	thaw	saw	lion	life	like
thorn	horn	torn	trees	treat	trim
lick	thick	big	move	pool	boom
show	grow	throw			

II. **Auditory Training:**
    A. paw — grandfather
    B. thorn — dreamed
    C. lick — hunting
    D. show — licked
    E. lion — pleased
    F. trees — started
    G. move — breakfast

III. **Q.I.E.:**
Present the word *stuck*.
Possible correct responses are —

stuck   A. A big thorn was stuck in the lion's paw.
stung   B. A bee stung the lion on his back.

IV. **Auditory Training:**
    A. A bee stung the lion on his back.
    B. A big thorn was stuck in the lion's paw.

V. **Sentence Exercises:**

stories   A. Andy's grandfather told him stories about hunting lions.
lion   B. Andy saw a lion behind a tree.
thorn   C. The lion had a thorn stuck in his paw.
pulled out   D. Andy pulled out the thorn with a pair of pliers.
licked   E. The lion licked Andy's face.

VI. **Auditory Training:**
    A. lion
    B. pulled out
    C. licked
    D. thorn
    E. stories

VII. **Story Exercises:**

Andy went to the library to get a book about lions. He took the book home and read and read. His grandfather told him stories about hunting lions. Andy dreamed all night long about lions. After breakfast he started off to school. He came to a turn in the road and saw something move in the trees. He went to look behind the big pine tree and saw a lion. The lion blocked his way when he started to run. The lion held out his paw to show him what was wrong. It was a big thorn stuck in his paw. Andy always carried a pair of pliers in his back pocket. He pulled out the thorn. The lion licked Andy's face to show how pleased he was.

VIII. **Auditory Training:**
    A. lion — lied
    B. stuck — stung
    C. lick — leak
    D. look — book
    E. paw — maw
    F. back — pack

MISSING PANTS

I. **Q.R.E.:**

INITIAL:			FINAL:		
wall	fall	tall	hole	hose	hope
stairs	bears	hairs	ran	raft	rag
wet	set	bet	came	cane	case
hole	pole	roll			

II. **Auditory Training:**
    A. wall — looked
    B. stairs — jumped
    C. wet — pulled
    D. hole — raining

E. ran — supper

F. came — puddle

III. **Q.I.E.:**

Present the word *pants*.

Possible correct responses are —

pass

bass

paints

pants	A. The boy's pants are wet.
pass	B. The quarterback threw a long pass.
bass	C. I caught two bass at the lake.
paints	D. He paints his bicycle every year.

IV. **Auditory Training:**

A. He paints his bicycle every year.

B. The quarterback threw a long pass.

C. The boy's pants are wet.

D. I caught two bass at the lake.

V. **Sentence Exercises:**

pants	A. The boy jumped in a puddle and got his pants wet.
took off	B. He ran home and took off his pants.
hung	C. He hung his pants on the wall.
dog	D. His dog came in and got his pants.
lost	E. The boy couldn't find his pants.

VI. **Auditory Training:**

A. took off

B. pants

C. dog

D. lost

E. hung

VII. **Story Exercises:**

One day a boy was on his way home to eat supper. It was raining, and there was some water in a hole. He jumped in the puddle and got his pants wet. He ran home and took off his pants. He hung his pants on the wall and went to the bathroom. His dog came in and pulled his pants off the wall. The dog ran downstairs and out the door. The boy came back to get his pants. He looked for them all over his room but couldn't find them. He thought his pants were lost. In a little while, his dog came running back through the house dragging his pants. Now, he knew where they were.

VIII. **Auditory Training:**
- A. pants — paints
- B. dog — log
- C. hole — hose
- D. came — same
- E. got — cot

MOUSE'S BIRTHDAY PARTY

I. **Q.R.E.:**

Initial:			Final:		
cream	beam	seam	made	maze	make
blow	slow	flow	cheese	cheap	cheat
sing	thing	wing	cake	came	cage

II. **Auditory Training:**
- A. cream — cannon
- B. blow — eating
- C. sing — birthday
- D. made — happen
- E. cheese — balloon
- F. cake — ice cream

III. **Q.I.E.:**

Present the word *popped.*

Possible correct responses are —

mopped

popped   A. The balloon popped when the pin hit it.

mopped   B. The lady mopped the kitchen three times in one day.

IV. **Auditory Training:**
- A. The lady mopped the kitchen three times in one day.
- B. The balloon popped when the pin hit it.

V. **Sentence Exercises:**

mouse   A. The mouse found some cheese in a mouse trap.

cheese   B. The cheese was his birthday cake.

ice cream   C. He made a wish for an ice cream cone.

birthday cake D. He blew out the candles on his birthday cake.

window   E. A birthday hat flew out the window.

VI. **Auditory Training:**
   A. birthday cake
   B. window
   C. mouse
   D. ice cream
   E. cheese

VII. **Story Exercises:**

A mouse stole some cheese from a mouse trap. He said, "This will make a good birthday cake for me." He took the cheese home to his family. They put candles on the cheese. The mouse blew out the candles and made a wish. He wished that he had an ice cream cone. When he blew out the candles, his brother's cap flew out the window. The cap fell on a bird. The bird hit a tree. An acorn fell off the tree. The acorn hit a woodpecker on the head. The woodpecker thought that the fire alarm hit him. He pecked on the fire alarm box. The fire truck came. The firemen got some water from a fish pond.

A cat and a frog were at the fish pond. The cat had a balloon. The cat let the balloon go and the frog tried to catch the balloon. A hunter saw the balloon and shot an arrow at it. The balloon popped, and some people heard the noise. They got a blanket and tried to catch the frog. A pig was holding the blanket. The pig's foot hit a see-saw. A ball was on the see-saw. The see-saw threw the ball up in the air. A turtle was getting some ice cream. The ball fell into the ice cream cone. The turtle dropped the ice cream cone. The ice cream landed in a cannon. The cannon fired. The ice cream fell on the mouse's table. The mouse got his birthday wish. Everybody ate the ice cream. They all sang "Happy Birthday to You".*

VIII. **Auditory Training:**
   A. cone — coat
   B. ice — kite
   C. cake — cage
   D. cheese — check
   E. popped — mopped

---

*Emberly, Ed.: *Birthday Wish*. Toronto, Little Brown, 1977.

NEW PET

Q.R.E.:

Initial:			Final:		
sit	bit	fit	leash	lead	leap
dog	fog	rock	wipe	white	wise
pet	set	vet			

II. **Auditory Training:**

A. sit — roll over   D. leash — barking

B. dog — ran away   E. wipe — dog house

C. pet — collar

III. **Q.I.E.:**

Present the word *pet*.

Possible correct responses are —

met

bet

pat

pet   A. I got a new pet for Christmas.

met   B. I met the dog catcher at the corner.

bet   C. I bet your puppy can't jump as high as mine.

pat   D. Don't pat strange dogs because they might bite you.

IV. **Auditory Training:**

A. Don't pat strange dogs because they might bite you.

B. I met the dog catcher at the corner.

C. I got a new pet for Christmas.

D. I bet your puppy can't jump as high as mine.

V. **Sentence Exercises:**

name   A. I thought of a good name for the puppy.

vet   B. I take my puppy to the animal doctor for shots.

homework   C. I must finish my homework before I get to play with my puppy.

vitamins   D. My puppy takes his vitamins better when I put them in his food.

tricks   E. My puppy is learning to jump over a fence.

VI. **Auditory Training:**
   A. vet
   B. vitamins
   C. tricks
   C. homework
   E. name

VII. **Story Exercises:**

My parents bought me a new puppy last week. I named him Floppy. Floppy is fuzzy, warm, and friendly. He is brown with white spots. He is small but will be very big when he grows up. He runs up to me when I walk into the house. He tries to jump up on me, but he is too little to jump very high. He likes for me to pick him up and play with him. I rub his ears and scratch his head. Floppy is so young that he misses his mother. We put a clock in his bed at night to keep him from barking. He never barks or cries when he has the clock.

VIII. **Auditory Training:**
   A. puppy — puppet
   B. brown — frown
   C. small — tall
   D. bed — beg
   E. grow — no

PARK

I. **Q.R.E.:**

	INITIAL:	
slide	hide	fried
kite	bite	light
chips	tips	trips

II. **Auditory Training:**
   A. slide — playground
   B. kite — flying
   C. chips — picnic

III. **Q.I.E.:**

Present the word *wind.*
Possible correct responses are —
wheel
week

went
win
wind　　　　　A. The wind is blowing hard today.
wheel　　　　B. The wheel is going around.
week　　　　　C. This week is movie week.
went　　　　　D. I went to see Santa Claus.
win　　　　　　E. I am going to win the prize.

IV. **Auditory Training:**
　　A. I went to see Santa Claus.
　　B. The wheel is going around.
　　C. The wind is blowing hard today.
　　D. I am going to win the prize.
　　E. The week is movie week.

V. **Sentence Exercises:**
　　monkey bars　A. I love to climb the monkey bars.
　　picnic　　　　B. We are having a picnic at the park.
　　slide　　　　C. The boy is going down the slide.
　　flying　　　　D. The man is flying the kite for the boy.
　　playground　E. We see-sawed at the playground.

VI. **Auditory Training:**
　　A. picnic
　　B. flying
　　C. slide
　　D. monkey bars
　　E. playground

VII. **Story Exercises:**
　　My mom and dad take me to the park on weekends. We eat a picnic lunch of chicken, potato salad, and bread. I always want Coke to drink. My dad flies my kite when the weather is nice.
　　I play with the kids on the playground. We go down the slide a lot. I love to climb the monkey bars. We walk in the water when it is hot. I always need a drink of water after I play hard.

VIII. **Auditory Training:**
　　A. fly — buy
　　B. park — dark
　　C. drink — think
　　D. walk — talk
　　E. climb — dime

PLAY HOUSE

I. **Q.R.E.:**

INITIAL:			FINAL:		
jump	thumb	bum	play	plan	blast
saw	thaw	claw	trees	dream	treat
two	blue	flew	man	pass	back

II. **Auditory Training:**
   A. jump — sawed
   B. saw — ladder
   C. two — every day
   D. play — hammer
   E. trees — windows
   F. man — tree house

III. **Q.I.E.:**
   Present the word *man*.
   Possible correct responses are —
   pan
   bat
   mat
   mail

man	A. The man gave the boy some boards.
pan	B. The pan is on the stove.
bat	C. The boy hit the ball over the fence and broke his bat.
mat	D. Please wipe your feet on the mat.
mail	E. The mailman brought me a letter today.

IV. **Auditory Training:**
   A. The boy hit the ball over the fence and broke his bat.
   B. The man gave the boy some boards.
   C. The pan is on the stove.
   D. Please wipe your feet on the mat.
   E. The mailman brought me a letter today.

V. **Sentence Exercises:**

plays	A. John plays with many of his friends.
play house	B. Bob and John decided to build a play house.

hammer	C. John got a hammer from his dad.
saw	D. Bob got a new saw from his dad.
door and	E. They made a door and two windows.
windows	

VI. **Auditory Training:**
   A. play house
   B. plays
   C. door and windows
   D. saw
   E. hammer

VII. **Story Exercises:**

John plays with many of his friends every day. He likes his friend Bob better than his other friends. Bob and John play basketball and baseball. Bob is John's best friend.

Bob and John decided to build a play house in a tree. A man gave them some boards and some nails. John got a hammer from his dad. Bob got a saw from his dad. They sawed the boards and nailed them together. They built a big play house. They made a door and two windows in their house. Bob made a ladder to climb up to the play house. They are proud of their new house.

VIII. **Auditory Training:**
   A. nail — tail
   B. ladder — fatter
   C. tree — trick
   D. door — roar
   E. dad — mad

PONY

I. **Q.R.E.:**

INITIAL:			FINAL:		
girl	pearl	whirl	ride	rise	ripe
spent	went	dent	took	tool	tooth
ring	sing	thing	show	shoe	she
stable	table	able	hug	hut	hum

II. **Auditory Training:**
   A. girl — animals
   B. spent — dressed

    C. ring — surprised
    D. stable — father
    E. ride — morning
    F. took — outside
    G. show — walked
    H. hug — up and down

III. **Q.I.E.:**

Present the word *pony.*

Possible correct responses are —

bony

money

body

pony	A. Linda went for a ride on a pony.
bony	B. John is so thin that people call him bony.
money	C. Do you have enough money for lunch today?
body	D. We exercise to build a good body.

IV. **Auditory Training:**
    A. John is so thin that people call him bony.
    B. Do you have enough money for lunch today?
    C. Linda went for a ride on a pony.
    D. We exercise to build a good body.

V. **Sentence Exercise:**

Linda	A. Linda loves all animals, but she likes ponies best.
pony	B. She rode a little pony at the fair one day.
horses	C. Linda's father let her ride one of his horses.
bought	D. Her father bought her a little black and white pony.

VI. **Auditory Training:**
    A. pony
    B. bought
    C. Linda
    D. horses

VII. **Story Exercises:**

Linda grew up on a small farm. She loved all of the animals

on the farm, but she loved horses best. One day she went to the fair and took a ride on a little pony. The pony walked around and around inside a tent. He was a lazy little pony, but she loved him. Linda asked her father to buy a pony for her birthday. Her father had horses on the farm, but he didn't have any ponies. Her father lets her ride the horses sometimes.

Her father took her to a horse show one day. They saw a little black and white pony. Linda fell in love with that pony. Her birthday was just one week away. She hoped her father would get that black and white pony for her. The next morning Linda got dressed and went to the stables. She opened the stable door and saw the little black and white pony. She was surprised. She ran and hugged her new pony.

VIII. **Auditory Training:**
    A. ring — rang
    B. let — led
    C. pony — bony
    D. stable — able
    E. hug — rug
    F. lot — let
    G. ride — right

SNOW

I. **Q.R.E.:**

INITIAL:			FINAL:		
woke	poke	soak	fort	form	force
snow	row	bow	bad	back	bath
ground	sound	found	road	rope	roast

II. **Auditory Training:**
    A. woke — snowman
    B. snow — fireplace
    C. ground — bird tracks
    D. fort — children
    E. bad — breakfast
    F. road — snowball

III. **Q.I.E.:**
Present the word *built*.
Possible correct responses are —
bill

mill
pill
bit
mend

built	A. The children built a snowman.
bill	B. The bill came for the firewood.
mill	C. The old sawmill is closed
pill	D. I took a pill for my cold.
bit	E. The dog bit the little boy.
mend	F. Mother will mend my gloves.

IV. **Auditory Training:**
  A. Mother will mend my gloves.
  B. I took a pill for my cold.
  C. The children built a snowman.
  D. The bill came for the firewood.
  E. The old sawmill is closed.
  F. The dog bit the little boy.

V. **Sentence Exercises:**

morning	A. I looked out the window this morning.
snow	B. There were five inches of snow.
mittens	C. I put on my coat and mittens.
frozen	D. The birdbath was frozen.
food	E. We threw out some bird food.

VI. **Auditory Training:**
  A. food
  B. snow
  C. morning
  D. mittens
  E. frozen

VII. **Story Exercises:**
One day Wendy woke up early in the morning. She looked out the window. Snow was all over the ground. Her mother made breakfast for her. She got dressed to go out and play. Her mother helped her put on her boots, coat, and gloves. Wendy went out to play. Some big children built a snowman in the yard next door. Wendy found a lot of tracks in the snow. There were small bird tracks under a tree. She saw some dog tracks and people tracks. Some of her friends were making a snow fort. A lot of boys threw snowballs across the road at them.

Wendy was getting cold. She went back in the house to warm up beside the fire.

VIII. **Auditory Training:**
    A. snow — blow
    B. cold — call
    C. fire — fight
    D. ball — hall
    E. road — boat

SWIMMING

I. **Q.R.E.:**

Initial:			Final:		
pool	fool	tool	game	gave	gaze
splash	flash	crash	dive	dies	died
float	boat	coat	put	push	purr
sun	fun	bun			

II. **Auditory Training:**
    A. pool — diving board   G. put — jump off
    B. splash — lifeguard
    C. float — shower
    D. sun — bathing suit
    E. game — cold water
    F. dive — swimming

III. **Q.I.E.:**

Present the word *pool.*
Possible correct responses are —
moon
pull
bull
put

pool	A. I go to the pool every day in the summer.
moon	B. The moon is pretty when it is full.
pull	C. The lifeguard pulled the girl out of the water.
bull	D. The bull got out of the pasture and chased me.

put E. We put on our fins and dove to the bottom.

IV. **Auditory Training:**
   A. We put on our fins and dove to the bottom.
   B. The moon is pretty when it is full.
   C. I go to the pool every day in the summer.
   D. The bull got out of the pasture and chased me.
   E. The lifeguard pulled the girl out of the water.

V. **Sentence Exercises:**
   water A. The water in the pool is beautiful.
   swimming B. I like to go swimming in the pool.
   waves C. There are no waves in a pool.
   float D. Do you know how to float?
   splash E. It is fun to splash water at the pool.

VI. **Auditory Training:**
   A. swimming
   B. float
   C. splash
   D. water
   E. waves

VII. **Story Exercises:**
   Tony is a little boy who loves to swim. He goes to the pool every day. He plays with his friends at the pool. They put on fins and dive to the bottom to look around. They float on their rafts and jump off the edge of the pool. One day Tony jumped into the water and splashed an old woman. The woman had on her best clothes. She got mad at Tony. The lifeguard made Tony stay out of the water for an hour. He was very sad.

VIII. **Auditory Training:**
   A. hour — out
   B. mad — map
   C. boy — toy
   D. raft — rat
   E. jump — pump

THREE LITTLE PIGS

I. Q.R.E.:

INITIAL:			FINAL:		
brick	stick	thick	ran	rag	rap
pig	twig	fig	huff	hug	hum
blow	grow	throw	big	bit	bib

II. Auditory Training:

A. brick — piggy
B. pig — brothers
C. blow — ever after
D. ran — smallest
E. huff — blow down
F. big — huff and puff

III. Q.I.E.:

Present the word *pig*.
Possible correct responses are —
big
pig A. The small pig ran to his brother's house.
big B. Have you ever seen a big bad wolf?

IV. Auditory Training:

A. Have you ever seen a big bad wolf?
B. The small pig ran to his brother's house.

V. Sentence Exercises:

three little pigs	A. Once upon a time there were three little pigs.
sticks	B. The first piggy built his house out of sticks.
straw	C. The next piggy built his house out of straw.
bricks	D. The smallest built his house out of bricks.
wolf	E. The wolf could not blow the brick house down.

VI. Auditory Training:

A. bricks
B. wolf
C. straw
D. sticks
E. three little pigs

VII. **Story Exercises:**

Once upon a time there were three little pigs. They were all brothers. The first piggy built his house out of sticks. The next piggy built his house out of straw. The smallest piggy built his house out of bricks. The big bad wolf came to the house made out of sticks. The wolf said, "I'll huff and puff and blow your house down." The wolf blew the house down. The little piggy ran to his brother's house. His house was made out of straw. The big wolf came to the house made out of straw. He said, "I'll huff and puff and blow the house down." The wolf blew the house down. Both little piggies ran to their brother's house. This house was made out of brick. The big bad wolf came to the brick house. He said, "I'll huff and puff and blow your house down." The wolf huffed and puffed, but he couldn't blow the brick house down. The three little piggies lived happily ever after.*

VIII. **Auditory Training:**
    A. wolf — hoof
    B. first — fist
    C. puff — huff
    D. brick — stick
    E. big — pig
    F. brother — mother

TREE HOUSE

I. **Q.R.E.:**

INITIAL:			FINAL:		
wood	could	stood	wall	wag	wash
build	killed	filled	rain	raise	rave
plan	stand	fan	roof	root	room
door	bore	four			
frame	tame	blame			
saw	paw	thaw			

II. **Auditory Training:**
    A. wood — hammer   D. door — roof top
    B. build — ladder   E. frame — measure
    C. plan — tree house   F. saw — carpenter

---

*Stobbs, William: *The Three Little Pigs.* New York, NcGraw. 1965.

        G. wall — to help
        H. rain — will not
    _ I. roof — some nails
III. **Q.I.E.:**
    Present the word *wood.*
    Possible correct responses are —
    wool
    would
    root

wood	A. We are building a tree house out of wood.
wool	B. I wear a wool sweater when it gets cold.
would	C. I would like to climb up the ladder.
root	D. A tree has roots that go deep into the ground.

IV. **Auditory Training:**
    A. We are building a tree house out of wood.
    B. I would like to climb up the ladder.
    C. A tree has roots that go deep into the ground.
    D. I wear a wool sweater when it gets cold.
V. **Sentence Exercises:**

build	A. We will build a tree house in the forest.
wood	B. We need wood and nails and tools to build a tree house.
roof	C. Our house will have a roof and a door.
measure	D. We need to measure the wood before we saw it.
hammer	E. We can all learn how to use a hammer.

VI. **Auditory Training:**
    A. wood
    B. roof
    C. hammer
    D. build
    E. measure

VII. Story Exercises:

We will build a tree house in the woods. We need long pieces of wood to build the tree house. We use the saw to cut the wood. We will need a hammer and some nails. The tree house will have walls, a door, and a roof. We will not get wet if it rains. Would you like to help us build a tree house?

VIII. Auditory Training:

A. nails — pails   D. piece — beasts
B. tree — free   E. door — floor
C. house — hot

TRIP TO THE LIBRARY

I. Q.R.E.:

INITIAL:			FINAL:		
book	hook	shook	bug	but	pup
page	gage	rage	took	toot	loop
moon	soon	stool	home	hole	hose
full	pull	wool			

II. Auditory Training:

A. book — library
B. page — finished
C. moon — showed
D. full — librarian
E. bug — joke book
F. took — to run
G. home — to look

III. Q.I.E.:

Present the word *moon*.
Possible correct responses are —
pool
boot
moon   A. The moon is bright yellow tonight.
pool   B. It is fun to play in a swimming pool.
boot   C. The boy stepped in a puddle and got
                   his boots wet.

IV. Auditory Training:

A. The boy stepped in a puddle and got his boots wet.
B. It it fun to play in a swimming pool.

C. The moon is bright yellow tonight.

V. **Sentence Exercises:**

moon	A. The boy found a good book about the moon.
mother	B. He let his mother look at the book.
joke book	C. The little boy wanted to find a joke book.
library	D. He finished the book and took it back to the library.
joke book	E. The boy found a joke book and took it home.

VI. **Auditory Training:**
- A. mother
- B. library
- C. joke book
- D. moon

VII. **Story Exercises:**

A little boy went to the library to get a book. He found a good book about the moon. The boy let his mother look at the book. He read the book outside until a bug flew on the page. He finished the book at school and took it back to the library.

The library was full of boys and girls. The little boy wanted to choose a joke book. The librarian showed him where to find a joke book. He found the joke book and took it home to read.

VIII. **Auditory Training:**
- A. get — gate
- B. bug — hug
- C. joke — jaw
- D. took — look
- E. library — librarian

WEATHER

I. **Q.R.E.:**

Initial:			Final:		
sun	fun	run	best	bet	beg
cold	sold	fold	fall	far	fast
snow	throw	grow	class	clap	clay

II. **Auditory Training:**

A. sun — weather   D. best — jack-o'-lantern
B. cold — warm and   E. fall — seasons
            sunny
C. snow — summer   F. class — winter

III. **Q.I.E.:**

Present the word *wind.*

Possible correct responses are —

will
win
wind   A. The wind blows my hat off every
               day.
will   B. I will buy you a new pair of boots.
win   C. That team always wins the game.

Present the word *fall.*

Possible correct responses are —

fought
fawn
fall   A. Farmers harvest their crops in the fall.
fought   B. Our football team fought the other
               players after the game.
fawn   C. A fawn is a baby deer.

IV. **Auditory Training:**

A. That team always wins the game.
B. The wind blows my hat off every day.
C. I will buy you a new pair of boots.
D. A fawn is a baby deer.
E. Our football team fought the other players after the
   game.
F. Farmers harvest their crops in the fall.

V. **Sentence Exercises:**

rain   A. It always rains a lot in April.
snow   B. I wear boots in the snow.
weather   C. Do you like cold weather?
sweat   D. Hot weather makes me sweat.
season   E. Fall is a very colorul and pretty
               season.

VI. **Auditory Training:**

A. weather
B. season

    C. snow

    D. sweat

    E. rain

VII. **Story Exercises:**

We learn about the weather in science class. There are four seasons of the year. Winter is cold. It snows sometimes. I wear a heavy coat and boots in winter. Spring is windy and wet. Flowers bloom in the spring. Summer weather is hot and sunny. I like to go swimming every day in the summer. Fall weather is cool. Leaves are colorful in the fall. We made a jack-o'-lantern in our class last fall. I like all of the seasons, but summer is the best time for me. Which season do you like best?

VIII. **Auditory Training:**

    A. sunny — funny

    B. swim — sweat

    C. time — type

    D. fall — tall

    E. leaves — leap

ZOO

I. **Q.R.E.:**

INITIAL:			FINAL:		
zoo	blue	two	bird	birth	purse
bear	fair	tear	cage	came	cake
tails	sails	fails	laugh	tap	tag

II. **Auditory Training:**

    A. zoo — kangaroo

    B. bear — giraffe

    C. tails — zoo keeper

    D. bird — bananas

    E. cage — monkeys

    F. laugh — animals

III. **Q.I.E.:**

Present the word *feed*.

Possible correct responses are —

feel

feet

feed   A. We can't feed the animals at the zoo.

feel   B. I like to feel the monkey's fur.
feet   C. The bear has big feet.
Present the word *lion.*
Possible correct responses are —
light
tight
lion   A. The lion roars when he sees a zebra.
light   B. The baby monkey had to have a light on every night.
tight   C. The lion tamer tied the rope very tightly around the lion's neck.

IV. **Auditory Training:**
  A. We can't feed the animals at the zoo.
  B. The bear has big feet.
  C. I like to feel the monkey's fur.
  D. The baby monkey had to have a light on every night.
  E. The lion roars when he sees a zebra.
  F. The lion tamer tied the rope very tightly around the lion's neck.

V. **Sentence Exercises:**
monkey   A. I watched the monkey swing from a branch.
zoo keeper B. The zoo keeper told us not to feed the animals.
pet and feed C. I like to pet and feed the animals at the petting zoo.
seals   D. Seals like to play in the water.
giraffe   E. The giraffe has a long neck and can see for miles.

VI. **Auditory Training:**
  A. zoo keeper
  B. giraffe
  C. pet and feed
  D. seals
  E. monkey

VII. **Story Exercises:**
Animals live at the zoo. There are bears, zebras, tigers, and lions. The bears are brown and fuzzy. Some bears are white. They live in a big cage. The monkeys are funny. They make me

laugh. They play on swings. They hang by their tails and eat bananas. Lions live in cages. They roar when people pass the cage. I am scared of lions. I like to go to the zoo. Do you like the zoo?

VIII. **Auditory Training:**
   A. zoo — boo
   B. bear — hair
   C. hang — hand
   D. roar — more
   E. lion — liar

Chapter 6

ADULT LESSON PLANS

Airplane Ride
Carpet Repair
Catalogue Order Clerk
Dental Hygienist
Dentist
Dog Kennel
Electrical Equipment
Electrician
Fishing
Flower Garden
Flower Show

Gardening
Golf
Hair Stylist
Janitor
Mechanical Drafting
Photographer
Picnic
Plumbing
Post Office
Pumping Gas

AIRPLANE RIDE

I. **Q.R.E.:**

INITIAL:			FINAL:		
seat	feet	meet	dove	toes	dope
ride	sight	hide	pave	bathe	page

II. **Auditory Training:**
   A. seat — airplane   C. dove — suitcase
   B. ride — captain   D. pave — parachute

III. **Q.I.E.:**
   Present the word *plane*.
   Possible correct responses are —
   plate
   plane   A. I flew in a plane to Washington, D.C.
   plate   B. I bought a plate with the Washington
              Monument on it.
   Present the word *ship*.
   Possible correct responses are —
   gyp
   chip
   ship   A. The stewardess called the plane a
              ship.
   gyp   B. The taxi driver tried to gyp me on the
              way to the airport.
   chip   C. The stewardess served us potato chips

and peanuts.

Present the word *bail*.

Possible correct responses are —

mail

male

bail	A. You need a parachute to bail out of a plane.
male	B. Pilots are usually male, but some may be female.
mail	C. Planes carry air mail letters and packages.

Present the word *gate*.

Possible correct responses are —

gain

| *gate* | A. Don't carry a gun through the gate. |
| *gain* | B. The pilot tried to gain time because he was late. |

IV. **Auditory Training:**

A. I bought a plate with the Washington Monument on it.

B. The taxi driver tried to gyp me on the way to the airport.

C. You need a parachute to bail out of a plane.

D. Planes carry air mail letters and packages.

E. The pilot tried to gain time because he was late.

F. Don't carry a gun through the gate.

G. Pilots are usually male, but some may be female.

H. The stewardess served us potato chips and peanuts.

I. I flew in a plane to Washington, D. C.

J. The stewardess called the plane a ship.

V. **Sentence Exercises:**

fly	A. I will take a plane to Washington, D. C. next week.
weigh	B. My baggage is always too heavy, and I have to pay extra.
bail	C. I hope we don't have to bail out of the plane.
ship	D. The stewardess called the plane a ship.

fat   E. My seat on the plane was beside a fat man.

VI. **Auditory Training:**
    A. fat
    B. fly
    C. weigh
    D. ship
    E. bail

VII. **Story Exercises:**

I flew on an airplane to Washington, D. C. last week. I packed my suitcase and took a bath before I left. I rode in a van to the airport. My ride was very bumpy. I arrived at the airport and boarded the plane. We flew off the runway and into the sky. The ride was very smooth. I wasn't afraid that we might have to bail out. I ate a delicious dinner on the plane. We landed safely in Washington, and I got through the gate without waiting a long time. My ride was fun.

VIII. **Auditory Training:**
    A. packed — back
    B. plane — main
    C. wait — wake
    D. sky — fly
    E. ate — gate

CARPET REPAIR

I. **Q.R.E.:**

INITIAL:			FINAL:		
tape	fame	same	tape	tail	take
rug	bug	tug	rug	rush	run
tight	fight	right	patch	pass	pad

II. **Auditory Training:**
    A. tape — ironing
    B. rug — padding
    C. tight — ruined
    D. patch — flooded

III. **Q.I.E.:**

Present the word *tight*.

Possible correct responses are —

tile
tide
light
lied
line

tight	A. It was a tight squeeze to get the carpet through the door.
tile	B. Water dripped on our tile floor.
light	C. My sister likes a light blue carpet.
lied	D. The manager of the store lied about how the carpet would be fixed.
line	E. I have called the manager several times, and the line is always busy.

IV. **Auditory Training:**
    A. My sister likes a light blue carpet.
    B. The manager of the store lied about how the carpet would be fixed.
    C. It was a tight squeeze to get the carpet through the door.
    D. I have called the manager several times, and the line is always busy.
    E. Water dripped on our tile floor.

V. **Sentence Exercises:**

apartment	A. Mrs. Williams lives in an apartment.
trouble	B. She has had a lot of trouble recently.
carpet	C. Water damaged her carpet last week.
carpet layer	D. She called a carpet layer to fix the carpet.
repaired	E. He patched her carpet and taped it in place.

VI. **Auditory Training:**
    A. carpet
    B. trouble
    C. repaired
    D. apartment
    E. carpet layer

VII. **Story Exercises:**

Mrs. Williams lives in an apartment. She has had a lot of trouble recently. The lady who lives upstairs always leaves her water running. Last Tuesday she went to work and left the water running in the bathtub all day. The tub ran over and leaked through Mrs. Williams' ceiling. The water got Mrs. Williams' carpet wet and damaged her sofa. Mrs. Williams called a carpet layer to check her carpet. The man came and told her that the carpet would need to be patched. It was really damaged from the flood. The man cut a new piece of carpet and taped it in place. He said, "This tape will make a tight fit." Mrs. Williams said, "Will you be able to fix my sofa?" The carpet layer said, "No, you should call a cleaning service."

VIII. **Auditory Training:**
    A. check — cheek
    B. said — sad
    C. tight — light
    D. place — lace
    E. wet — went

CATALOGUE ORDER CLERK

I. **Q.R.E.:**

INITIAL:			FINAL:		
size	flies	rise	ten	tick	tip
weight	freight	mate	pant	palm	pass
blue	true	glue	cash	cat	calm

II. **Auditory Training:**
    A. size — deliver
    B. weight — order
    C. blue — package
    D. ten — address
    E. pant — anything
    F. cash — number

III. **Q.I.E.:**
Present the word *ten*.
Possible correct responses are —
den
net
let
tell
ten   A. That will be ten dollars, please.

    den   B. Bears sleep in a den.

    net   C. The hair net keeps my hair in place.

    let   D. Please let me order two more of those.

    tell   E. I will tell you how to fix your hair.

IV. **Auditory Training:**
   A. Bears sleep in a den.
   B. Please let me order two more of those.
   C. That will be ten dollars, please.
   D. I will tell you how to fix your hair.
   E. The hair net keeps my hair in place.

V. **Sentence Exercises:**

  item   A. That package is too large an item to mail.

  size   B. I need a size ten in that pair of pants.

  postage   C. How much is the postage on that box?

  deliver   D. When can I expect you to deliver this order?

  order   E. The coat that I want to order is on page 435 in the sale book.

VI. **Auditory Training:**
   A. postage
   B. order
   C. size
   D. deliver
   E. item

VII. **Story Exercises:**

"Héllo, may I take your order?" "Yes, I want to order a pant suit." "What is your name and address?" "My name is Marta Baucom. My address is 527 North Oak St." "What page is it on in the sale book?" "It's on page 435." "What is the order number?" "The number is 4865-D." "What size do you want?" "I need a size ten, and I want blue." "How much will it cost with postage and tax added?" "It will be $75.00 plus $1.70 for postage and $3.00 tax. That will be $79.70 in all." "Do you want this cash or charge?" "I'll write a check for it. Do you think it will be delivered by Friday?" "Yes, you should get it by Friday. Will there be anything else?"

VIII. **Auditory Training:**

A. size — wise
B. cost — cot
C. number — tumbler
D. order — shorter
E. name — tame

DENTAL HYGIENIST

I. **Q.R.E.:**

INITIAL:			FINAL:		
bite	fight	white	teeth	team	tease
chin	thin	pin	tooth	tube	tool
pull	full	wool	lip	live	lid

II. **Auditory Training:**
   A. bite — dentist
   B. chin — cavity
   C. pull — filled
   D. teeth — toothpaste
   E. tooth — candy
   F. lip — yesterday

III. **Q.I.E.:**
   Present the word *bit*.
   Possible correct responses are —
   mit
   pit
   bill
   bid

   bit   A. The little boy bit the dentist's finger.
   mit   B. The little boy didn't get a new catcher's mit.
   pit   C. We cooked hamburgers on the B.B.Q. grill.
   bill   D. The dentist's bill was forty-five dollars.
   bid   E. My partner bid two hearts, and I passed.

IV. **Auditory Training:**
   A. The little boy didn't get a new catcher's mit.
   B. My partner bid two hearts, and I passed.

C. The little boy bit the dentist's finger.

D. We cooked hamburgers on the B.B.Q. grill.

E. The dentist's bill was forty-five dollars.

V. **Sentence Exercises:**

toothache	A. My tooth hurts when I eat something cold.
checkup	B. I visit my dentist twice a year for a checkup.
toothpaste	C. I need a new tube of toothpaste.
cavities	D. The dentist filled all of my cavities.
candy	E. Candy is not good for your teeth.
brush	F. You should brush your teeth after every meal.
toothbrush	G. My toothbrush is yellow.
ouch	H. The dentist pulled my tooth.

VI. **Auditory Training:**

A. checkup

B. toothpaste

C. toothache

D. cavities

E. brush

F. ouch

G. candy

H. toothbrush

VII. **Story Exercises:**

I went to the dentist yesterday. I had a bad toothache. The dentist said I had a big cavity. The dentist filled the cavity, and I felt better. He told me not to eat a lot of sweets. The dental hygienist cleaned my teeth. She gave me a new toothbrush and tube of toothpaste. She showed me the right way to brush my teeth. She said to brush after every meal. I learned how to care for my teeth at the dentist's office.

VIII. **Auditory Training:**

A. told — sold

B. felt — fit

C. me — my

D. clean — green

E. sweets — seats

F. teeth — tease

G. brush — slush

DENTIST

I. **Q.R.E.:**

Initial:			Final:		
went	sent	bend	floss	flock	flop
brush	flush	thrush	teeth	team	lean
seven	heaven	weaved	check	cheap	cheat
said	wet	fled			

II. **Auditory Training:**
   A. went — dentist
   B. brush — appointment
   C. seven — receptionist
   D. said — Johnson
   E. floss — cavities
   F. teeth — refused
   G. check — brushed

III. **Q.I.E.:**
Present the word *teeth.*
Possible correct responses are —
death
teeth   A. My teeth are full of cavities.
death   B. Do you fear death?

IV. **Auditory Training:**
   A. Do you fear death?
   B. My teeth are full of cavities.

V. **Sentence Exercises:**

dentist   A. Mrs. Johnson went to the dentist last June.

cleaned   B. The dentist cleaned her teeth.

cavities   C. He told her that she had seven cavities.

appointments   D. She made three appointments to have her cavities filled.

sweets   E. Mrs. Johnson is not eating any more cakes or pies.

VI. **Auditory Training:**
   A. appointments

    B. cleaned
    C. cavities
    D. sweets
    E. dentist

VII. **Story Exercises:**

Mrs. Johnson went to the dentist last June to have her teeth cleaned. The dentist checked her teeth after they were cleaned. He said, "You have seven cavities." Mrs. Johnson said, "I don't understand why I have so many cavities. I have brushed my teeth every day and used dental floss." The dentist told her to make three appointments to have the cavities filled. She stopped at the receptionist's desk and said, "I want to make some appointments." The receptionist said, "We have one appointment for July 5th. Will that date be O.K. for you?" Mrs. Johnson said, "Yes, but I need two other appointments." The receptionist asked her if July 16th and July 18th would be O.K. Mrs. Johnson said, "Yes, if I can get another appointment changed they will be fine." Mrs. Johnson went home and told her husband that she refused to bake any more cakes or pies.

VIII. **Auditory Training:**
    A. teeth — death
    B. floss — toss
    C. filled — filed
    D. yes — yet
    E. pies — buys

DOG KENNEL

I. **Q.R.E.:**

INITIAL:			FINAL:		
board	ford	stored	bath	bat	pack
price	slice	mice	leave	lean	leak
poodle	noodle	strudel	bag	ball	bash
place	face	race			

II. **Auditory Training:**
    A. board — kennel   E. bath — toenails
    B. price — special   F. leave — Friday
    C. poodle — clipped   G. bag — around
    D. place — following

III. **Q.I.E.:**
Present the word *bath*.
Possible correct responses are —
path
math

bath	A. Please give my dog a bath while he is here.
path	B. There was a long path around the kennel.
math	C. My grades in the math course were good.

Present the word *food*.
Possible correct responses are —

food	A. Do you have canned dog food?
foot	B. My dog hurt his foot last week.
fool	C. I never try to fool my brother on April Fool's Day.

IV. **Auditory Training:**
  A. My grades in the math course were good.
  B. Do you have canned dog food?
  C. I never try to fool my brother on April Fool's Day.
  D. Please give my dog a bath while he is here.
  E. My dog hurt his foot last week.
  F. There was a long path around the kennel.

V. **Sentence Exercises:**

board	A. I want to board my dog here for a week.
price	B. How much do you charge for a week?
food	C. I have special food for him to eat.
fence	D. Do you have a fenced in lot for him to run in?
bath	E. I want you to give him a bath while he is here.

VI. **Auditory Training:**
  A. price
  B. food
  C. fence
  D. bath
  E. board

VII. **Story Exercises:**

I would like to board my dog for a week. He is a French poodle. I want to have him bathed and his toenails clipped while he is here. I want him to eat only this food. The food is in this bag. I hope the price isn't too much. Do you have a lot for him to run around in? This place seems fine for him. I'll bring him next Friday and leave him until the following Friday.

VIII. **Auditory Training:**

    A. food — fool C. eat — seat   E. dog — dodge

    B. bag — beg   D. fine — file

ELECTRICAL EQUIPMENT

I. **Q.R.E.:**

INITIAL:			FINAL:		
power	tower	shower	post	poke	pole
crank	prank	drank	bleed	bleak	bleep
case	face	pace			

II. **Auditory Training:**

    A. power — electrical

    B. crank — chemical

    C. case — dip header

    D. post — residue

    E. bleed — neutralized

III. **Q.I.E.:**

Present the word *dip.*

Possible correct responses are —

tip

dim

limb

lip

dip	A. One piece of electrical equipment is called a dip-header.
tip	B. That man's name is on the tip of my tongue.
dim	C. You should dim your lights when you meet another car.
limb	D. The ice storm broke off the large limb on that tree.

    lip   E. I bit my lip, and it hurts.

IV. **Auditory Training:**
- A. I bit my lip, and it hurts.
- B. One piece of electrical equipment is called a dip-header.
- C. You should dim your lights when you meet another car.
- D. That man's name is on the tip of my tongue.
- E. The ice storm broke off the large limb on that tree.

V. **Sentence Exercises:**

parts   A. There are many different electrical parts.

Ph tests   B. Ph tests are performed on the towers.

algae tests   C. Algae build-up tests are performed on the towers.

residue   D. Chemical residue collects in the cooling towers.

neutralized E. The chemicals must be neutralized after they are used.

VI. **Auditory Training:**
- A. Ph tests   D. algae tests
- B. residue   E. neutralized
- C. parts

VII. **Story Excercises:**

Preventive maintenance is an important job. One man is assigned to the air compressors. It is his job to service them. He looks for oil in the crankcase and the oilers. He must also bleed the compressors of excess oil. The excess oil passes through the pistons, and the oil ends up in the crankcase. It is then collected.

VIII. **Auditory Training:**
- A. oil — soil
- B. crank — crane
- C. end — send
- D. bleed — feed
- E. air — hair

ELECTRICIAN

I. **Q.R.E.:**

INITIAL:			FINAL:		
wire	fire	tire	pipe	pike	pile
plug	rug	slug	job	jot	jog
drill	thrill	shrill	wire	wise	wife
bender	sender	fender			
short	court	fort			

II. **Auditory Training:**
   A. wire — electrician
   B. plug — breaker
   C. drill — lightening
   D. bender — service
   E. short — finished
   F. pipe — ten o'clock
   G. job — everything
   H. wire — tester

III. **Q.I.E.:**
   Present the word *bend*.
   Possible correct responses are —
   mend
   bent
   meant
   men
   pen

   bend   A. The helper bends the pipe for the electrician.
   mend   B. Cowboys mend fences so cows won't get out.
   bent   C. He bent the pipe so much that it broke.
   meant   D. He meant to call the electrician but forgot his number.
   men   E. All of the men worked overtime last week.
   pen   F. May I borrow your pen?

IV. **Auditory Training:**
   A. Cowboys mend fences so cows won't get out.
   B. The helper bends the pipe for the electrician.

C. All of the men worked overtime last week.

D. May I borrow your pen?

E. He bent the pipe so much that it broke.

F. He meant to call the electrician but forgot his number.

V. Sentence Exercises:

bend	A. Please put a ninety degree angle in the pipe.
pull	B. He wore blisters on his hands when he tried to pull the wire.
short	C. He looked and looked but couldn't find the short in the wire.
work	D. They knocked it out in about one hour.
shock	E. Be careful! It will burn you.
change	F. They had to change the service.
conduit	G. He ran thirty feet of pipe this morning.
panel	H. Who put on the wrong panel cover?
straps	I. That pipe has to be strapped up.
knock out	J. The hole in the box was too big, so we had to use some reducing washers.

VI. Auditory Training:

A. short	F. shock
B. pull	G. strape
C. bend	H. knock out
D. conduit	I. work
E. change	J. panel

VII. Story Exercises:

The electrician went to bed last night about ten o'clock. He woke up about three in the morning because someone called him. They wanted him to fix their fuse box because lightning struck their house and shorted everything out. He went to their house and put in some circuit breakers. He forgot his tester, so he wasn't sure which breaker to use. Nothing was burned up so he was safe. He would have to change the service, so he left it like it was. He went back the next day and finished the job.

VIII. Auditory Training:

A. bed — bead
B. tester — fester
C. burned — learned
D. fix — tricks
E. three — tree

FISHING

I. **Q.R.E.:**

INITIAL:			FINAL:		
boat	vote	wrote	bite	bike	pipe
fish	wish	dish	pass	mat	bath
hook	shook	look	hook	hood	hoof

II. **Auditory Training:**
   A. boat — duck pond   D. bite — fishing
   B. fish — motor boat   E. pass — sleeping
   C. hook — fisherman   F. hook — travel

III. **Q.I.E.:**
   Present the word *wet.*
   Possible correct responses are —
   went
   rent

   wet   A. I try to wet a hook at least once a
             week.
   went   B. I went to the sporting goods store yes-
             terday to buy some hooks.
   rent   C. I want to rent a boat for the day.

IV. **Auditory Training:**
   A. I try to wet a hook at least once a week.
   B. I want to rent a boat for the day.
   C. I went to the sporting goods store yesterday to buy
      some hooks.

V. **Sentence Exercises:**
   fishing   A. I go fishing every time I get a chance.
   wish   B. I wish I could go fishing every day.
   boat   C. I rented a boat at the pier for ten dol-
             lars.
   pond   D. My fish pond at home is too small for
             large fish.
   hooked   E. I hooked a big one, but he got away.

VI. **Auditory Training:**
   A. hooked
   B. wish
   C. pond
   D. boat
   E. fishing
VII. **Story Exercises:**
   Fishing is a lazy man's sport. Some fishermen may not agree that fishing is a lazy way to pass the day. They may be more serious about fishing than I am. They spend more money than I do and work to find the best fishing spot. They travel for miles to find good fishing holes. They may sell their fish and make lots of money. I fish by the bank of a pond and don't try to look for good holes. I don't use a rod and reel. I tie a hook on a string and tie it to my toe. I lie down and rest and wait for the fish to bite. I have fun fishing and sleeping.
VIII. **Auditory Training:**
   A. money — sunny
   B. bank — sank
   C. mile — might
   D. bite — fight
   E. fish — fifth

FLOWER GARDEN

I. **Q.R.E.:**

INITIAL:			FINAL:		
weed	bead	seed	stung	stuff	stump
bite	light	fight	brave	break	brain
bees	trees	sees	tall	tar	tap

II. **Auditory Training:**
   A. weed — fertilizer
   B. bite — watering can
   C. bees — blossoms
   D. stung — beehive
   E. brave — greenhouse
   F. tall — careful
III. **Q.I.E.:**
   Present the word *seed.*

Possible correct responses are —

seat

seen

seal

scene

seed	A. I will plant a bean seed in a cup.
seat	B. The usher helped me find my seat.
seen	C. I have never seen flowers grow so fast.
seal	D. The prettiest rose gets a blue seal for first place.
scene	E. Do you want to use my plants in the garden scene?

IV. Auditory Training:

A. The prettiest rose gets a blue seal for first prize.

B. The usher helped me find my seat.

C. I have never seen flowers grow so fast.

D. Do you want to use my plants in the garden scene?

E. I will plant a bean seed in a cup.

V. Sentence Exercises:

weeds	A. Weeds always grow faster than flowers.
violets	B. Violets are easy to grow in small pots in the house.
dew	C. The morning dew helps water flowers.
sun and rain	D. Plants need sun and rain to make them grow.
fertilizer	E. Don't put too much fertilizer on young plants

VI. Auditory Training:

A. dew

B. weeds

C. violets

D. sun and rain

E. fertilizer

VII. Story Exercises:

I planted some flower seeds in the garden last spring. The seeds came up fast, and the plants grew very tall. The flowers are blooming now, and they are pretty. Some blossoms are red, and some are yellow. Our backyard smells good because of all of the flowers. Bees fly around in our yard. The bees pollinate the flowers and sting people who aren't careful. I got stung once and had to put some alcohol on it.

VIII. **Auditory Training:**
  A. flower — power
  B. cry — fry
  C. tall — fall
  D. fly — try
  E. yard — yarn

FLOWER SHOW

I. **Q.R.E.:**

INITIAL:			FINAL:		
win	tin	pin	leaf	lead	leap
rule	fool	pool	win	wig	wish
judge	fudge	budge	rule	roof	room
bloom	room	fume	niche	nip	nick

II. **Auditory Training:**
  A. win — garden
  B. rule — restaurant
  C. judge — coliseum
  D. bloom — council
  E. leaf — African
  F. win — violet
  G. rule — schedule
  H. niche — ribbons

III. **Q.I.E.:**
  Present the word *plant.*
  Possible correct responses are —

  plant   A. I always plant my garden on Good Friday.

  plaid   B. My pants are plaid, and my coat is a solid color.

  plan   C. Do you plan to go to the flower show at the Coliseum?

  bland   D. The food at that restaurant is bland.

IV. **Auditory Training:**

A. I always plant my garden on Good Friday.
B. The food at that restaurant is bland.
C. Do you plan to go to the flower show at the Coliseum?
D. My pants are plaid, and my coat is a solid color.

V. **Sentence Exercises:**

flower show	A. The garden club is having a flower show next week.
arrangement	B. A good arrangement wins a blue ribbon.
judges	C. The flower show judges choose the winners.
horticulture	D. Cut specimens are displayed in Coke bottles.
creativity	E. Creativity is important in flower arrangements.

VI. **Auditory Training:**
   A. arrangement
   B. horticulture
   C. creativity
   D. judges
   E. flower show

VII. **Story Exercises:**

The Council of Garden Clubs is having a flower show. The flower show schedule lists the classes for arrangements. Mary is going to make an arrangement. She will call the entry chairman to register. The class she chose requires fresh plant material. She needs a water supply. The flowers are held in place by needlepoint. Mary will show the arrangement in a niche.

Mary wants to show horticulture, too. She will show her African violet. She will label it with the botanical name. The leaves are very healthy. Live flowers are in bloom. The soil must not show. The pot must be clean. The flower show judges will choose the winners. Mary hopes she will win two blue ribbons.

VIII. **Auditory Training:**
   A. show — shoe
   B. soil — toil

C. win — ween
D. flower — floors
E. pot — pod
F. name — lame

GARDENING

I. **Q.R.E.:**

INITIAL:			FINAL:		
shade	made	fade	seed	seem	seek
time	rhyme	crime	plant	plank	place
seed	bead	weed	limbs	list	link
flower	tower	shower			

II. **Auditory Training:**
   A. shade — vegetables
   B. time — pruned
   C. seed — lettuce
   D. flower — biennials
   E. seed — tomatoes
   F. plant — removed
   G. limbs — flowering

III. **Q.I.E.:**
   Present the word *lime.*
   Possible correct responses are —
   time
   dime

   lime   A. Lime is used on plants to make the soil sweet.

   time   B. Gardening takes a lot of time, but it is rewarding.

   dime   C. You need to spend more than a dime to buy a plant.

IV. **Auditory Training:**
   A. Gardening takes a lot of time, but it is rewarding.
   B. Lime is used on plants to make the soil sweet.
   C. You need to spend more than a dime to buy a plant.

V. **Sentence Exercises:**
   vegetable   A. These vegetables are fresh from the garden.

shrub	B. Shrubs make very good ground cover.
order	C. I want to order my flower seed early this spring.
bulbs	D. I ordered my bulbs from the seed catalogue.
prune	E. We pruned the bushes in front of the house.

VI. **Auditory Training:**
  A. order
  B. bulb
  C. prune
  D. vegetable
  E. shrub

VII. **Story Exercises:**

You must work hard in your garden in August. Late summer is a good time to prune shade trees. Dead limbs are easily seen and removed then. Shrub pruning should be done then, also. New growth will hide pruning wounds. You should not prune azaleas, because you would cut off next year's buds.

This is the time to plant a late vegetable garden. You can plant late tomatoes now. You can also plant broccoli, carrots, and lettuce. You can plant flower seeds, too. Perennials and biennials can be planted now. Make plans for planting spring-flowers buds. (From the *Greensboro Daily Newspaper*.)

VIII. **Auditory Training:**
  A. prune — prude
  B. perennials — biennials
  C. seed — seek
  D. buds — buns
  E. time — lime

GOLF

I. **Q.R.E.:**

INITIAL:			FINAL:		
win	chin	thin	green	Greek	grease
middle	fiddle	little	sand	same	safe
show	grow	snow	hit	him	hiss
money	honey	funny			

II. **Auditory Training:**
   A. win — hundred   E. green — favorite
   B. middle — tournament F. sand — middle
   C. show — golfer   G. hit — Palmer
   D. money — fairway
III. **Q.I.E.:**
   Present the word *fan.*
   Possible correct responses are —
   van
   fat
   fad
   fan   A. The golf pro had five hundred fans at the last tournament.
   van   B. The golf shop delivers supplies in a large van.
   fat   C. It's hard to hit a golf ball when you are too fat.
   fad   D. The fad now is to wear plaid golf pants.
IV. **Auditory Training:**
   A. The golf shop delivers supplies in a large van.
   B. The fad now is to wear plaid golf pants.
   C. The golf pro had five hundred fans at the last tournament.
   D. It's hard to hit a golf ball when you are too fat.
V. **Sentence Exercises:**
   tournament   A. I watched the golf tournament on T.V. last night.
   favorite   B. Do you have a favorite golf club to use on the green?
   money   C. Palmer won $50,000.00 during the last tournament.
   fairway   D. A pro golfer always hits the ball down the middle of the fairway.
   fan   E. Are you a golf fan?
VI. **Auditory Training:**
   A. money
   B. fairway
   C. favorite

D. fan

E. tournament

VII. **Story Exercises:**

I watched the golf tournament on T.V. yesterday. Those pros can swing so easily. They are always down the middle of the fairway. They never land in a sand trap. That is how to win big money. Palmer, Miller, Weiskoph, and Nicklaus are the top pros. They put on some show at the last tournament. Jack Nicklaus won the tournament, but Palmer is the fan's favorite. Who is your favorite?

VIII. **Auditory Training:**

    A. pros — bows

    B. won — sun

    C. fan — van

    D. swing — sing

    E. show — sew

    F. money — honey

HAIR STYLIST

I. **Q.R.E.:**

INITIAL:			FINAL:		
dry	fry	pry	rinse	rent	rim
blow	flow	glow	comb	call	cough
part	dart	cart	wedge	web	wet
tint	mint	vent			

II. **Auditory Training:**

    A. dry — damaged   E. rinse — beauty shop

    B. blow — shampoo   F. comb — conditioned

    C. part — appointment G. wedge — brushed

    D. tint — blow dry

III. **Q.I.E.:**

Present the word *set.*

Possible correct responses are —

said

sell

sale

send

set   A. I want to have my hair set in a different way.

said	B. The stylist said my hair had been damaged.
sell	C. I am not planning to sell my house.
sale	D. The sale price for the shampoo and blow dry is $4.95.
send	E. Will you send me a notice about my next appointment?

IV. **Auditory Training:**
   A. Will you send me a notice about my next appointment?
   B. The stylist said my hair had been damaged.
   C. I am not planning to sell my house.
   D. I want to have my hair set in a different way.
   E. The sale price for the shampoo and blow dry is $4.95.

V. **Sentence Exercises:**

appointment	A. The customer made an appointment for a shampoo and a blow dry.
curling iron	B. She asked me to use the curling iron on her bangs.
cut	C. Do you want me to cut your hair in a different style this time?
wash and cut	D. I shampooed her hair and cut it in a wedge.
precision cut	E. My last customer wanted a precision cut with long bangs.

VI. **Auditory Training:**
   A. curling iron
   B. wash and cut
   C. precision cut
   D. appointment
   E. cut

VII. **Story Exercises:**

The customer got to the beauty shop just in time for her 2:00 appointment. She walked to a chair in the back and spoke to her male hair stylist. She sat down in the reclining chair and laid her head in the sink. She relaxed there as her hair was shampooed and conditioned. Her hair stylist dried her hair with a large towel. She followed him to a different chair, and he blow dried and brushed her hair into shape. She thanked the hair stylist as she paid him and left.

VIII. **Auditory Training:**
- A. chair — share
- B. shape — shake
- C. male — made
- D. sat — set
- E. head — heat

JANITOR

I. **Q.R.E.:**

INITIAL:			FINAL:		
fix	picks	six	cough	cause	caught
pants	dance	chance	like	life	lies
bank	thank	sank	work	worth	worse
shirt	hurt	dirt			

II. **Auditory Training:**
- A. fix — machine
- B. pants — whistle
- C. bank — trailer
- D. shirt — factory
- E. cough — connection
- F. like — workers
- G. work — old clothes

III. **Q.I.E.:**

Present the word *tool.*

Possible correct responses are —

tune

toot

noon

tool	A. I use a tool to clean the machine.
tune	B. I heard a good tune on my radio.
toot	C. The whistle toots when it's time for lunch.
noon	D. We stop working at noon for lunch.

IV. **Auditory Training:**
- A. I heard a good tune on my radio.
- B. I use a tool to clean the machine.
- C. We stop working at noon for lunch.
- D. The whistle toots when it's time for lunch.

V. **Sentence Exercises:**

money	A. I cash my check on Friday.
pants	B. I paid fifteen dollars for work pants last week.

music　　　　C. I listen to music at work on my radio.

driver's license D. I left work to take my driver's license
test yesterday.

VI. **Auditory Training:**
   A. pants
   B. driver's license
   C. music
   D. money

VII. **Story Exercises:**

I get up to go to work at 5:30 in the morning. My trailer is
far from the factory. I drive my car like a race car driver to make
it to work on time. When I get to work, I clean machines. The
way I clean machines is to sweep the dirt from the connection
points. The factory workers thank me and go to work making
tools.

I have to wear old clothes that can get dirty. I bought a shirt
and pants for work at the Family Dollar store. I use my pay-
check for clothes and my bills. Life is good to me because I
have a car, a trailer and my music.

VIII. **Auditory Training:**
   A. like — life
   B. dirt — hurt
   C. race — raise
   D. sweep — sweet
   E. bills — pills

MECHANICAL DRAFTING

I. **Q.R.E.:**

INITIAL:			FINAL:		
paper	shaper	taper	ink	it	is
parts	darts	hearts	draft	drag	drab
lead	fed	bed	type	tile	dye
draw	paw	straw			

II. **Auditory Training:**
   A. paper — drafting　　E. ink — millum
   B. parts — mechanical　F. draft — materials
   C. lead — vellum　　　G. type — simpler
   D. draw — plastic

III. **Q.I.E.:**
Present the word *lead.*
Possible correct responses are —
dead
debt
den

lead	A. Plastic lead is used on vellum.
dead	B. The policeman discovered that the man had been dead for two weeks.
debt	C. My debts every month are more than I earn.
den	D. Bears live in a den.

IV. **Auditory Training:**
A. My debts every month are more than I earn.
B. Bears live in a den.
C. Plastic lead is used on vellum.
D. The policeman discovered that the man had been dead for two weeks.

V. **Sentence Exercises:**

picture	A. I copy from pictures and partial pictures at work.
machines	B. It is important to understand machinery in my line of work.
angles and tilts	C. Drafting tables can be adjusted to different angles and tilts.
vellum	D. Plastic lead is used on vellum.
millum	E. Millum is a special kind of paper.

VI. **Auditory Training:**
A. machines
B. vellum
C. millum
D. angles and tilts
E. picture

VII. **Story Exercises:**
A mechanical draftsman details parts of machines. They must draw exactly. The parts are made from these drawings. He can copy the part from a picture, partial picture, verbal description, or the part itself. He can also design the part himself.

Draftsmen draw on different materials. Vellum is a type of plastic. It is simpler to draw on than paper. Plastic lead is used on vellum. Lead pencils are used on regular paper. Millum is a specific type of paper. Ink is used on it. Ink can be used on vellum too.

VIII. **Auditory Training:**
    A. paper — taper
    B. ink — end
    C. lead — bed
    D. part — smart
    E. draw — straw

PHOTOGRAPHER

I. **Q.R.E.:**

INITIAL:			FINAL:		
light	fight	sight	print	prize	prime
print	flint	lint	rough	rub	rush
dens	wins	sins	light	lime	like

II. **Auditory Training:**
    A. light — photographed   E. print — negative
    B. print — chemicals   F. rough — recorded
    C. dens — invisible   G. light — processed

III. **Q.I.E.:**
Present the word *lens.*
Possible correct responses are —
dens
tens
tense

lens	A. Light shines through the camera lens and exposes the film.
dens	B. Bears live in dens all winter.
tens	C. The saleslady gave me two tens for a twenty-dollar bill.
tense	D. Students are always tense before exams.

IV. **Auditory Training:**
    A. Bears live in dens all winter.

  B. Light shines through the camera lens.
  C. Students are always tense before exams.
  D. The saleslady gave me two tens for a twenty-dollar bill.

 V. **Sentence Exercises:**

picture	A. Photographs are fun to take.
film	B. Negatives are sensitive to light.
exposure	C. You shoot the picture after it is composed properly.
print	D. The paper has an invisible image.

 VI. **Auditory Training:**
  A. picture
  B. exposure
  C. print
  D. film

VII. **Story Exercises:**

The negative is used to make a photographic print. The print looks just like the world you photographed. Prints are made by shining light through the negative onto a sheet of paper that is light sensitive. The paper holds an invisible image from the light shining through the camera lens. The light sensitive paper is processed in chemicals. The same chemicals are used to process your film. The picture you shot now becomes visible. The negative is a picture of the light recorded on film. The print is a picture of light recorded on photographic printing paper. Light is what we see with our eyes. Light is what we use to make photographs.

VIII. **Auditory Training:**
  A. shot — shoot
  B. light — like
  C. print — lint
  D. picture — mixture
  E. process — processed

PICNIC

 I. **Q.R.E.:**

INITIAL:			FINAL:		
lake	cake	bake	day	date	lame

sun	fun	run	fork	fort	fours
knives	wives	hives	both	bowl	bows
tea	see	me	sail	self	says

II. **Auditory Training:**
   A. lake — macaroni
   B. sun — Sunday School
   C. knives — beautiful
   D. tea — chicken
   E. day — delicious
   F. fork — swimming
   G. both — afternoon
   H. sail — badminton

III. **Q.I.E.:**
   Present the word *sauce*.
   Possible correct responses are —
   saws
   sows
   sews

sauce	A. The chicken was good with barbecue sauce.
saws	B. The man saws wood with a chain saw.
sows	C. The farmer sows turnip seeds in early spring.
sews	D. My wife sews a new dress for every new occasion.

IV. **Auditory Training:**
   A. The man saws wood with a chain saw.
   B. The chicken was good with barbecue sauce.
   C. My wife sews a new dress for every occasion.
   D. The farmer sows turnip seeds in early spring.

V. **Sentence Exercises:**

picnic	A. My Sunday School class went on a picnic.
games	B. We played badminton and softball all morning.
food	C. We ate chicken and macaroni salad for lunch.
lake	D. We went swimming and sailing in the

afternoon.

trip   E. We had a great time on our trip to the
                       lake.

VI. **Auditory Training:**
   A. food
   B. games
   C. trip
   D. picnic
   E. lake

VII. **Story Exercises:**

My Sunday School class went on a picnic to the lake last
week. It was a beautiful day for a picnic. We played badminton
and softball in the morning. My side won both games. The
teacher forgot to bring forks and knives, but we managed with
our fingers. The chicken was good with barbecue sauce. The
macaroni salad was delicious too. I drank coffee, but some
people drank tea. That afternoon we went swimming. I got
sunburned and had to buy some lotion. My friend went sailing
on the lake. All of us had a great time on our trip to the lake.

VIII. **Auditory Training:**
   A. went — win
   B. forks — forts
   C. tea — tie
   D. lake — late
   E. sauce — saws
   F. fingers — lingers
   G. outing — scouting

PLUMBING

I. **Q.R.E.:**

INITIAL:				FINAL:	
leak	peak	streak	cost	cob	cough
fuse	loose	choose	fix	fit	film
heater	cheater	meter	hot	hock	hob

II. **Auditory Training:**
   A. leak — washer
   B. fuse — circuit
   C. heater — blow
   D. cost — Thompson

E. fix — located

F. hot — element

III. **Q.I.E.:**

Present the word *tap.*

Possible correct responses are —

tamp

lap

lamp

tap	A. Will you put a new washer in the tap?
tamp	B. The plumber always tamps the dirt back after he digs a ditch.
lap	C. The football player ran three laps around the track.
lamp	D. I need a new shade for the lamp in the den.

IV. **Auditory Training:**

A. Will you put a new washer in the tap?

B. I need a new shade for the lamp in the den.

C. The plumber always tamps the dirt back after he digs a ditch.

D. The football player ran three laps around the track.

V. **Sentence Exercises:**

batch feed	A. I installed a new batch feed disposal for her.
faucet	B. The faucet in the bathroom has been dripping for two months.
channel locks	C. Channel locks are used to take out a faucet stem.
ball cock	D. A ball cock is used in a commode.
close coupling gasket	E. A close coupling gasket should fit tight so the commode won't leak.

VI. **Story Exercises:**

"Hello, are you Mrs. Thompson? I'm the plumber. I understand you are having trouble with your hot water heater. Where is it located?" "It's in the basement." "Is it blowing fuses, or do you have circuit breakers?" "We don't have fuses, but it has thrown the circuit breaker four times." "Is it leaking?" "I haven't seen any water running out." "How old is your water heater?" "I think it's about twelve years old."

"Mrs. Thompson, I checked the water heater, and the lower element is burned out. Do you want me to go ahead and fix it?" "Yes, but how much will that cost me?" "It will be approximately $64.00." "While you're here I also want you to check the commode upstairs."

VIII. **Auditory Training:**
- A. hot — pot
- B. check — cheat
- C. old — sold
- D. water — wetter
- E. basement — casement

POST OFFICE

I. **Q.R.E.:**

Initial:			Final:		
stamp	lamp	cramp	zip	sit	seek
letter	setter	fetter	book	boot	boom
bills	wills	tills	late	lake	tame

II. **Auditory Training:**
- A. stamp — vacation
- B. letter — Veterans Day.
- C. bills — stamp machine
- D. zip — post office
- E. book — holidays
- F. late — closed

III. **Q.I.E.:**

Present the word *mail.*

Possible correct responses are —

bail

pail

paid

mail	A. Will you mail this letter for me today?
bail	B. The judge set the robber's bail at $50,000.
pail	C. The old woman carried a pail of water to the garden.
paid	D. I paid the fine for the parking ticket.

IV. **Auditory Training:**

A. I paid the fine for the parking ticket.
B. The old woman carried a pail of water.
C. Will you mail this letter for me today?
D. The judge set the robber's bail at $50,000.

V. **Sentence Exercises:**

package	A. I sent a package C.O.D. to my friend in Florida.
zip code	B. You must put the zip code on everything you mail.
special delivery	C. I insured the letter and sent it special delivery.
book rate	D. Books may be mailed for less if you send them book rate.
Christmas	E. The post office wants you to mail letters and packages early for Christmas.

VI. **Auditory Training:**
   A. special delivery
   B. book rate
   C. Christmas
   D. zip code
   E. package

VII. **Story Exercises:**

I went to the post office to buy stamps. I can't believe they cost so much these days. I was in a hurry to get my mail off because my bills were due. When I pulled on the post office door it was locked. I saw a sign that said "Closed for Veterans Day." The government employees have so many holidays. I am a vet, and I don't get a vacation on Veterans Day. I finally decided to go get change and buy my stamps from a stamp machine. I hope my bills will not be late because the post office was closed.

VIII. **Auditory Training:**
   A. cost — coast
   B. bills — pills
   C. buy — pie
   D. stamp — stab
   E. mail — pail

PUMPING GAS

I. **Q.R.E.:**

Initial:			Final:		
car	bar	far	half	hat	ham
cold	bold	told	gas	gap	gag
pay	day	say	cash	cap	can

II. **Auditory Training:**
   A. car — register
   B. cold — gas pump
   C. pay — oil stick
   D. half — money
   E. gas — antifreeze
   F. cash — pressure

III. **Q.I.E.:**

Present the word *paid*.
Possible correct responses are —
pail
pain
bail
bait
mail
made
main
mate

paid	A. I paid for my gas before I pumped it.
pail	B. They won't let you put gas in a plastic pail.
pain	C. I felt a pain in my chest last night.
bail	D. My son got arrested, and I had to bail him out.
bait	E. I got some worms to use for fish bait.
mail	F. My tax refund is coming in the mail.
made	G. I made too much money and had to pay taxes.
main	H. The main thing I wanted was gas for my car.
mate	I. I lost the mate to my sock.

IV. **Auditory Training:**

A. They won't let you put gas in a plastic pail.

B. My son got arrested and I had to bail him out.

C. My tax refund is coming in the mail.

D. I made too much money and had to pay taxes.

E. The main thing I wanted was gas for my car.

F. I lost the mate to my sock.

G. I paid for my gas before I pumped it.

H I felt a pain in my chest last night.

I. I got some worms to use for fish bait.

V. Sentence Exercises:

gas lines	A. The gas lines were very long today.
oil	B. I remembered to look at my oil stick.
pressure	C. The air pressure in my tires was low.
antifreeze	D. My antifreeze was good for fifteen below zero.
unleaded	E. Most new cars use unleaded gasoline.

VI. Auditory Training:

A. oil

B. unleaded

C. pressure

D. gas lines

E. antifreeze

VII. Story Exercises:

I pulled up to the pump and stopped my car. I went inside to pay for the gas. The lady said, "Remember to stop pumping at half the price." I paid her. I didn't understand what that meant and asked her to explain. She told me that the pump didn't register high enough these days because gas was $1.08 per gallon. I knew I should begin to drive less and get into a car pool for work.

VIII. Auditory Training:

A. pump — bump

B. gas — cash

C. car — can

D. oil — boil

E. line — time

Chapter 7

SUGGESTIONS FOR
DEVELOPING ADDITIONAL PLANS

1. Observe and/or talk to children to obtain material for additional plans. Interview adults to obtain samples of common terms used in connection with their hobbies, sports, etc. Terminology used in conjunction with an adult's occupation may also be used. Refer to the interview forms in Appendix A and B since these interview forms could be used as guides and for developing additional lesson plans.
2. Consider the individual's residual hearing, speechreading ability, language level, and signing skills when writing material.
3. Q.R.E. should be constructed so that the initial or final consonant visibly differentiates between the words. For example, /p/, /f/, and /w/ in the initial position of pull, full, and wool are different enough in movement to clearly differentiate between these words. The /p/, /v/, and /d/ in the final position of lip, live, and lid are different enough in movement to clearly differentiate between these words. Vowel sounds in the words may be varied slightly since adjacent vowels have similar movements. See Appendix C.
4. The Auditory Training material following Q.R.E. should be developed by selecting the first word from each of the lines of Q.R.E. words and contrasting that word with a two syllable word or a multisyllabic word from the story.
5. Q.I.E. requires selection of a word that has other possible words that are homophenous to it. One syllable words are easier than two syllable words for this type of material. For example, in using the word *pat* the following combinations may be formed — bat, mat, pet, pan, ban, man, pad, bad, mad, men, etc. Proper names are not usually good choices. However, credit must be given if a name is received in response to (A) in Q.I.E. Nonsense words are unacceptable

even though homophenous. See Appendix C.

6. Auditory Training materials following Q.I.E. should be developed by scrambling the same sentences used in the Q.I.E. The homophenous words are not used because they are too difficult for this step in the training program.

7. Write all sentences using the following rules proposed by Streng*:

   a. Sentences should be made up largely of visible articulatory hovements. The visibility should be distributed evenly throughout the sentence.

   b. There should be definite contrast between successive articulatory movements in a sentence.

   c. The more visible the verb, the easier the sentence is to understand.

   d. Alliteration should be avoided.

   e. Sentences should be of moderate length. Short ones do not carry enough meaning. Long ones are too difficult to remember.

   f. Sentences should evoke a definite word picture.

   g. It is easier to lipread a sentence which observes simple order, as subject-verb-object-modifiers, than one which begins with a clause.

   h. A rhythmic sentence is easier to read than one in which modifiers or parenthetical expressions are interposed between the main parts of the sentence.

   i. Verbs in the active voice are easier to understand than those in the passive voice.

8. Auditory Training materials following Sentence Exercises are developed by scrambling the clue words used for the sentences.

9. Write stories to comply with Streng's rules (1969, p.206) for stories:

   a. A story should be logically organized, one sentence leading into the next, the whole being divided into no more than 2 paragraphs and consisting of from 8 to 15 visibly constructed sentences. (Stories for young children should be short but still coherent and have a point.)

   b. A story may or may not contain conversation.

---

*From Alice Streng, *Hearing Therapy for Children*, 2d edition, 1969, p. 205-207. By permission of Grune & Stratton, New York.

    c. Biography, history, geography and science make good sentence material but poor story material. A single episode or anecdote which has the characteristics noted in 1 and 2 above about a person or event makes a satisfactory story.

    d. Inclusion of a great number of proper names makes the discourse more difficult to understand.

    e. If a tale or long story is read, it should be phrased in visible language but should not be condensed so as to take the charm out of the original. This type of material lends itself to the seeing-hearing types of presentation, rather than to lip reading alone.

10. Auditory Training material following the story exercise should show a progression to more difficult material. Words are selected from the story and contrasted with other words that have minimal distinctive feature differences.

Chapter 8

DATA COLLECTION

IN keeping with current trends, the authors find that a data collection system aids the instructor in recording and determining therapy progress. Delores Butt's *Speechreading Test For Children* or Utley's *Speechreading Test For Adults* may be used as a pretest to determine the beginning level of difficulty for speechreading material. The pretest in *Apple Tree or Developmental Sentence Analysis* by Laura Lee may be used to determine the beginning language level.

The following data collection form was designed to be used during each lesson so that tracking of responses can be converted into percentages. The obtained percentages can be compared from day to day so that progress may be charted or graphed and presented as a report to students and parents. Data collection also reminds the instructor when an easier or more difficult task should be attempted. As a rule of thumb, it is suggested that a criterion of no less than 80 percent accuracy be maintained at a task level to ensure success, and when 95 percent accuracy level is achieved a more difficult task step should be introduced.

DATA COLLECTION

Name_____

Date_____

	1	2	3	4	5	6	7	8	9	10		Total # responses	Total # incorrect	Total # correct	% correct
I D											X				
E											X				
II C											X				
III A											X				
B											X				
E											X				
IV B											X				
V C											X				
D											X				
VI B											X				
VII D											X				
VIII B											X				

CODE: + = correct

- = incorrect

Appendix A

INTERVIEWS — ADULT

AMP CORPORATION — ELECTRICAL EQUIPMENT

OUR operation consists of the *maintenance* crew arriving at the plant ten minutes prior to operation of the shift. I arrive beforehand to look over and oversee the problems we might have facing us on that particular day. One man is assigned to do *preventive maintenance* on both the *100 horsepower, 75 horsepower,* and the *20 horsepower air compressors.* It's his job, every day, to service these compressors for oils used in the *crankcase* and the *oilers* and also to *bleed* down the compressors of excess oil that has passed through the *pistons* back to the crankcase. Another man is assigned to service and to chemically analyze the *cooling towers* at every shift. This man performs *Ph tests* on the towers, *algae build-up* tests, and also blows the towers down for chemical residue collecting in the bottom of these towers. At this point he will add whatever chemicals may be necessary to neutralize the Ph factors in the towers to bring them up to a 6.5 to 6.8 level of *neutralization.* These towers are used in operation of process for *molding injection equipment* and also for cooling tower purposes and for cooling air compressors. Another man's responsibility would be to check the *boiler* daily. At this point he would record outside temperature, time on the hour meter, and he would record how many gallons of oil were used per shift or per day. At this point all men would report to the *plant manager.*

Daily problems might exist first in the injection molding department. This department consists of automated injection molding machines, conveying equipment to transport materials to a grinder, and a pull-back system in which to incorporate pulling back ground-up material as it has been injected through the molding machine. This material consists of four different colors of what we generally refer to as virgin and regrind. The material at this point is pulled through the pull-back system through a separator, which consists of a wire screen being driven by a motor. The fines at this point are separated out of the material to prevent a buildup of static electricity in the metal lines. Generally, this is one of the most common breakdowns we face each day.

The injection molding machines consist of high temperature and high hydraulic pressure. The carriage of the machine opens — closes — injects (to 1500 PSI) — cycles — the mold opens — the sweep comes down or the hydraulic injectors, whichever the case may be, knocks the parts off of the mold, down the shoot to the conveyor — they are transported by the conveyor into the parts separator — the good parts are deposited in a box — the runner or left injection process is carried into the grinder — it is ground up and pulled back by the pull-back system. These machines are all solid state — electrically operated. The detailed information about operation consists of heater drivers, thermocouples, and hydraulic motors. The injection process is controlled by solid state DC drive boards and timer boards.

If molding is in operating capacity, there may be problems with assembly equipment, which comes in forms of dip-header parts, post-header parts, or break-switch parts. These machines are fully automated and will run by themselves, but there has to be an operator to constantly monitor two machines per operator.

The break-switch machines consist of housings — plastic housings that are inserted into a machine along with a bottom plunger — a spring — a top plunger — and a cap. These machines roll on a turntable. As the part comes around, a certain amount of pressure is applied. It is checked for clearances usually from 1/30th to 1/36,000th of an inch. If the part is good and the spring check reads good, it injects the part into the good parts bin. If the part is bad, it rejects the part into the defective parts bin. Generally, we try to run no more than a 22 percent bad parts bin. If for some reason it is over or under that, parts are checked for tolerance to be sure that the parts are good when they go into the machines. The post-header equipment consists of one operator for two machines — inserting metal pins in plastic strips at certain intervals. These intervals may be from 1/7th to 1/27,000th of an inch. These parts, after pins are inserted, go into another part of assembly, in which they are inserted into a plastic housing to make a terminal connector.

CATALOGUE ORDER CLERK

First you say, "May I help you"? Then you listen to their complaint. If they want to write a check for more than twenty-five dollars, you have to have it approved by a superviosr. To get her there, you have to page her. Also you have to constantly watch for shoplifters. And if you see one you have to call on the 'phone. It seems like you have to dial Code 7 or something. I don't know what else to say. If you're gonna have a job where you have to stand up, I learned you have to wear comfortable shoes. There are different kinds of ways to ring things up on a register. Layaways are the most difficult. It takes several different forms that you have to fill out. Then if you don't ring it up right — we have the computerized kinds of registers — so that if you make a mistake, you have to void it while the customer is standing there impatiently. And right after Christmas is the worst time. If the customer wants to exchange something, they have to go to the business office and get it approved and then come back to the register. We have these little places called stations where the cash registers are. I did work in the shoe department for a while. Well, when I worked there, I did the register there, looked for shoe sizes, and answered the telephone. Let me tell you it was a thrilling experience. To open a register, the first thing you do is put your employee number in, then you put the date in, the type of purchase is coded on the sales slip, and then you put that in the register, and from then on it flashes up on the screen what you're supposed to do next.

DENTAL HYGIENIST

What is a dental hygienist?

A dental hygientist's primary concern is prevention of cavities and peridontal diseases. This means not only in the

office but in doing such things as visiting schools.
Routine day.

8:30 — the day starts. I see six patients in the morning. Then I break for an hour lunch. In the afternoon I see four more patients.

What is the main function of the dental hygienist?

I clean teeth, examine and mark down things that the dentist should look at, take x rays, give fluoride treatments, and help the dental assistant.

What is the difference between the dental assistant and the dental hygienist?

The dental assistant sets up for each procedure, hands the instruments to the dentist, mixes preparations, cleans up afterward, and gets paid a lot less.

Can you describe an average visit of a patient?

By now, I know most of the patients so I usually start a conversation about whatever they do, etc. I then ask if they are having any problems with their teeth — toothaches, etc. After that I take a quick check in their mouth and inform the dentist. The dentist takes a look himself and tells me the treatment plan. This might include full mouth x rays and cleaning, or a full series of x rays and a full cleaning, or just cleaning, etc. After that the patient is scheduled for a complete examination that includes x rays and oral examination (charting).

What are some of the phrases that you use while working on a patient?

"Spit." "Would you like to spit that out?" or "O.K., would you empty that?" "Close just a little." "Open wider." "Tilt your head back like you're looking at the ceiling." "Bite down on the x ray tab."

How would you describe to a patient the correct way to brush his teeth?

It's really hard to describe it without demonstrating. You aim the bristles up toward your gum so that the bristles get into the little cuff around your tooth. Then you jiggle the brush. This dislodges the plaque and food debris. Do not cross brush because you can wear a grove in the root. After the gum recedes, the root, which is not covered by enamel, is exposed.

What do you mean by gum recession, yuck!

Gum recession is a part of the aging process of the individual. The amount of recession depends on the person's age,
heredity, and tooth-brushing method.

ELECTRICIAN

What is your occupation?

Electrical contractor and electrician.

What do you do in your everday work as an electrician?

Well, we get a lot of trouble calls. Now we've become
"trouble shooters." We go to a house and have to find a
"short" in a wall, up in the attic, or sometimes in the
ground. We install "service poles" for mobile homes; change
services in houses and businesses; wire new homes, tobacco
barns, air conditioners, and billboards. During the summer
we keep up maintenance of the rides at the amusement areas.

What kinds of tools are required?

No electrician should be without a pair of "kleins" or side-
cutters. He should also have a good sharp knife, Phillips and
regular screwdrivers (two or three), channel locks, and black
tape. For the bigger tools we use pipe benders, pipe
threaders, ditch-digging machines, drills, hole cutters (hydraulic), etc.

What else do you do?

We change "ballasts" in fluorescent lights, change the tubes,
change fixtures, recepticles (plugs), switches, and panels. On
new jobs we run pipe and wire, if it's a big job. Many times
we call the pipe conduit and the wire by its size. For example, 12-2, 14-2, Romex®, etc.

What about the materials?

Like I said, we have different size wire; 10-2, 12-2, 14-2, and
Romex are the most common. Pipe comes in sizes of 1/2 inch
and 3/4 inch up to 4 inches. Then there are the connectors,
fittings, reducing washers, boxes, scotch locks (or wire
weights), anchors, sheet metal, screws, breakers, fuses, straps,
steel (snake-to-pull wire), plug and switch covers (brown and
ivory), lug bolts, etc.

Vocabulary

		Idioms
conduit	short	"put a 90. . ."
wire	Romex®	"pull wire"
fixture	kleins	"run pipe (conduit)"
ballasts	knife	"skin the wire"
panels	channel locks	"change the breaker"
breakers	screw driver	"knock it out in ___"
fuses	Phillips	"it will burn you"
connectors	bender	"change the service"
fitting	drill	"put it up"
reducing washers	wire nuts	"burn it up"
boxes (box)	Pipe (10ft.)	"shorted out"
screws	rigid (pipe)	"trouble shoot"
straps	EMT (conduit)	
steel (snake)	circuit	
plugs	shock	
switches	bushing	
covers	tester	

HAIRSTYLIST

The term we are most commonly called by is "hairstylist."

Most women come in once a week for a set. She will tell us if she wants a half bang, down on the forehead, or quarter bang. She tells us if she wants it turned under or up in the back. In a cut, we generally slither, taper, or layer the hair. Most often we taper with a set. A razor cut is one in which we roll the short and long ends together for more volume and height without much teasing.

At the beauty school you nan get a shampoo, cut, and blow-dry for $6.50.

We can give a precision cut in response to a picture. She can just bring a picture and show us how she wnts it cut. In considering the cut, it's very important to be aware of the features. For example, we do not want to hide the eyes. With large eyes we want the hair away — to accent the eyes. For me, it's important to consider the jawline. With a distinctive jawline, you'd want short sideburns or none at all.

We do a dry set by using a curling iron. A dry set is like a wet roller but much faster. We blow-dry the hair first. Often we use a round brush. We have scalp treatments for dandruff control. If the customer wants added body we can give a body wave. For more curl, we can also do a permanent wave. We can change hair color, frost the hair, and tint. Highlighting is popular now. Call and set up an appointment.

Lingo

cut	layer	curling iron
set	razor cut	dry set
half or quarter bang	tease	permanent
wedge	shampoo	color
frost	blow-dry	tint
color	cream rinse	roll
slither	conditioner	highlight
taper	precision cut	body wave

MECHANICAL DRAFTSMAN

I work with machines. I detail each part so somebody could produce it from my drawing. You must draw it exactly. You can either copy the part from a picture, partial picture, instructions, or the part itself, or the other alternative is to design the part yourself. The company I work for builds air compressors. I would think, on the average, there are many plants of this type all over the world. I am also called a detailed draftsman. Draftsmen should have considerable knowledge concerning the machine's operations. This way it will be easier for me and other draftsmen to design parts that would work in the simplest way. The key here is simplicity.

Types of draftsmen:

Technical illustrators — drawings show the order in which things are put together but are without dimensions. They do not draw to scale, but they merely draw to proportion, which allows them to draw faster.

Electrical draftsmen — draw circuit boards and electrical diagrams.

Architect draftsmen — draw houses and landscape.

Pipe draftsmen — design different pipes for large companies.

Structural steel draftsmen — design I-Beams for large buildings.

How much do you rely on your speech?

I've got to understand the part I'm drawing. Sometimes you

don't get a picture or even a partial picture. I have to rely on a description given to me verbally by the design draftsman. I come into verbal contact with the design draftsman the most. During my working day the only person I need to come into verbal contact with is my boss who often has things for me to do. However, I'd like to stress the importance of the relationship between the designer or design draftsman and myself. It is essential I understand exactly what he wants, or a lot of time will be wasted.

There is considerable terminology that could only be covered with more extensive study. These terms are a few of the many, but these are some of the basic ones. In the U. S. we look at objects in the third angle projection to draw them. In England they use first angle projection, which is the reverse of the way we draw.

Terms:

compass

protractor

erasing shield — a little piece of tin with different holes and different lines so that I can put it on that line or that hole and erase it without erasing everything surrounding it.

electric eraser — they make things a lot faster and a lot neater. You have your scale. See, sometimes you don't draw on full scale. You draw on 1/2 scale, 1/4 scale, 1/8 scale. 1/8 scale — smallest we ever draw.

templates — plastic with different size circles that are used to draw your circles instead of using your compass. You see, these are in even increments, and if the circle you need is not an even increment, you need to use your compass.

ellipse template

welding template — sometimes you work with metals so you have to weld them together. You have to let someone know how you want it welded so you use welding symbols from your template. Different symbols mean different ways to weld. You draw these on your drawing and then draw an arrow to that point needing welding.

blueprints — used every day to send people copies of our work. There are different substances you can draw on. I'm using paper now, but when I worked at Gravely, I used vellum.

vellum — plastic, and it is so much easier to draw on than paper. Plastic lead is used on vellum, with regular paper, lead pencils.

lead pencils — I use three different sized lead pencils.

microfilm — we always keep the original copy, and this is also microfilmed. At Gravely we only had one individual part on a sheet of paper. Now at Ingersoll—Rand I put as many different parts as possible on one page. I don't like this way because spacing becomes an important consideration.

reference material — used to find out as much as we can about the different parts and different engines offered by the various companies. Representatives are sent from these companies advertising their parts or engines.

french curves — another template; it has weld angles or curves. It is a flat piece of plastic cut into the various curves.

drafting pad — little bag of powder that picks up your loose graphite (lead). This powder is sprinkled on your drawing and brushed off with a drafting brush.

drafting table — different drafting tables do various things. Some have better tilts and angles than others.

sanding block pad or file — these are used to sharpen your lead. These will sharpen your pencils to a very fine point.

dividers

adjustable triangles

millum — another kind of paper. Ink is used on this type.

tolerance — this is the exact size you want something.

clearance — for example, take a hole and an iron rod. The hole must be larger than the rod, and this difference in space is the clearance. You draw things in sections if the part is too large to draw on the paper or if the other sections of the part are identical. You draw in full section, half section, and quarter sections.

hidden lines — refer to the lines that are not visible but must be added to your drawing for it to be accurate.

stretch out — for example, say you have a u-shaped piece of metal. Because it is u-shaped, it has 290 degree bends. What I would draw is this metal not bent or stretched out. But the one consideration with a stretch out is that when a metal is bent, it stretches, so in order to get certain lengths in the bent view you start off with a piece of metal smaller than all three sides added together. These values are predetermined. The outer edge of your drawing should stand out as soon as you look at the drawing. The hidden lines should be slightly lighter and slightly finer.

lighter lines — lines of the outermost edge.

dimension lines — arrows that tell you the exact length of the piece. The dimension lines should be roughly the same thickness and darkness as the hidden lines. The outer edge, which is your hold line, is made with a soft lead pencil.

INTERVIEWS — CHILDREN

DANCING CLASS

What is your name?

_____

How old are you?
  Seven and a half.
Where do you go to school?
  Derita Elementary.
What grade are you in?
  Second.
Tell me about a day at school.
  We have a TV. I go to watch TV. Then we have a playtime,
  and then math, and then lunch.
What do you do after lunch?
  We have a rest period. Then we do a story or go to a special
  class.
What kind of special class?
  PE, library, or music. Then we pack up our books in our
  satchels and go home.
What do you do in the afternoon?
  Oh, I study and watch TV and play games.
Tell me who you like to watch on TV or read about.
  I like to read about Juliet Lowe.
  Who is that?
  She is the founder of Girl Scouts.
Are you a Girl Scout?
  Um huh!
Tell me about Girl Scouts.
  We do a lot of fun things. Like play games or do a lot of fun
  things. Or sing or do the flag ceremony.
How often do you meet?
  Every Tuesday.
Who do you like to watch on TV?
  "Hardy Boys."

Who is in it?

Shaun Cassidy and Parker Stevenson. Shaun is 19, and Parker is 20. They are around that age.

Why do you like them?

I just like the Hardy Boys.

What else do you like to do?

Well, I collect turtles.

What kind of turtles?

Not real ones, you've seen them.

How many do you have?

I haven't counted 'em in a while because I've got two shelves of 'em.

What are your hobbies?

Well, I like to paint and sing and dance and that's all.

Do you take dancing lessons?

Yes, there are twelve in the class. There are six, seven, eight, and nine year olds in the class.

What kind of dance do you take?

Tap and ballet.

Which do you like better?

Tap. Well, it's sort of clogging.

Who teaches your class?

Miss Sherry, Miss Debbie, and Miss Sandra. Miss Sandra teaches acrobatics; it's not like dance, it's like an exercise class. And Miss Debbie and Miss Sherry teach tap and ballet.

Is that your baby?

Yes, but she's a doll.

What's her name?

Pussycat. Santa Claus brought her. P-U-S-S-Y-C-A-T.

Did you go to church this morning?

Yes, well the preacher's sermon wasn't so good.

Why?

Well, it just wasn't so good. That's all I think I have to say.

But tell me about your pet.

How did you know I had a dog?

I've seen her. Tell me about her.

She's black and gray and white, and she loves the snow and ice. She plays with me.

What's her name?

Buffy. Your boots are so soft. I like them.

Tell me about your mother's new car.

It's red. I have to go now.

Appendix C

THE VISIBLE COMPONENTS
OF THE SPEECH SOUNDS*

Sᴘᴇᴇᴄʜʀᴇᴀᴅɪɴɢ is based on the movements and positions of the lips, tongue and teeth which, when seen, help differentiate the sounds of speech.

The consonant sounds of speech may be divided into four groups as follows:

I.   Those formed and revealed by the lips.

(p,b,m,) A. The "p" sound, as in "pay," "apple," and "soup;" the "b" sound, as in "bat," "table," and "rub;" and the "m" sound, as in "meat," "hammer," and "jam" may be identified by the movement of the lips opening from a closed position.

(f,v)   B. The "f" sound, as in "father," "after," and "cough," and the "v" sound, as in "very," "ever," and "leave," may be identified by the movement of the lower lip to the upper teeth.

(w,wh) C. The "w" sound, as in "way," and "anyway," and the "wh" sound, as in "what" and "everywhere," may be identified by the lips being drawn together or puckered.

II.   Those formed by the tongue and revealed by the lips.

(r)   A. The "r" sound, as in "run," and "around," may be identified by the lips drawing together or puckering at the corners.

(s,z)   B. The "s" sound, as in "some," "sat," and "say," and the "z" sound as in "zero," "razor," and "fuzz," may be identified by the teeth being very close together and the lips extended with the opening narrow.

(ʃ,ʒ,) C. The "sh" sound, as in "shut," "bashful," and

*From pages 46-48 in *New Lessons in Lip Reading* by Elizabeth Helm Nitchie (J.B. Lippincott Company). Copyright 1950 by Elizabeth H. Nitchie. Reprinted by permission of Harper & Row, Publishers, Inc.

142

(tʃ,dʒ) "plush;" and the "zh" sound, as in "vision" and "garage;" the "ch" sound, as in "chimney," "patchwork," and "rich;" and the "j" sound, as in "jury," "major, and "page," may be identified by the lips thrust forward or projected.

III. Those formed and revealed by the tongue.

(θ,ɣ) A. The "th" sound, as in "thumb," "bathtub," and "forth," and the voiced "th" sound, as in "this," "brother," and "bathe," may be identified by the point of the tongue showing between the teeth or just behind the upper teeth.

† (1) B. The "l" sound, as in "look," "alive," and "bell," may be identified by the movement of the tongue tip leaving the upper gum.

(t,d,n) C. The "t" sound, as in "time," "matter," and "sat;" the "d" sound, as in "desk," "lady," and "bed;" and the "n" sound, as in "now," "any," and "bone," may be identified by the flat edge of the tongue touching the upper gum. The teeth are close together, making the movement difficult to see.

IV. Those revealed largely by context.

(k,g) A. The "k" sound, as in "keep," "baker," and "luck," and the "g" sound, as in "go," "finger," and "big," may be identified by the slight drawing up on the muscles above the Adam's apple. The movement is very slight, and frequently the sounds must be in-dentified from context.

(j) B. The "y" sound, as in "you" and "loyal," may be identified by the relaxed position of the lips and the narrow lip opening but must frequently be identi-fied from context.

(h) C. The "h" sound, as in "who" and "anyhow," con-tains no movement and must be obtained from the context.

The vowel sounds of speech may be identified on the basis of the shape of the lips and the degree of opening between the lips. It should be noted that we are referring to the vowel

---

†May be included with (t,d,n)

sounds, not the vowel letters of the alphabet.

Width of   Shape of Lips
Opening

	Puckered	Relaxed	Extended
Narrow	chew, boot, group	it, wish, milk	eat, beet, sea
Medium	book, full, wool	other, jump, us	any, get, guess
Wide	awful, call, paw	army, got, pop	ashes, ran, tack

The diphthong (sound made up of a combination of two vowel sounds) may be divided into two groups as follows:
  I. Those with puckered final movements.
    A. The "ow" sound, as in "owl," "mouse," and "how." Relaxed-wide followed by a puckered movement.
    B. The "o" sound, as in "o" sound, as in "old," "boat," and "flow."
  Contracting-puckered movement.
    C. The ū sound as in "mute." Relaxed-narrow and puckered narrow.
  II. Those with relaxed-narrow final movements.
    A. The "i" sound, as in "i̱deal," and "pi̱pe," and "by̱." Relaxed-wide and relaxed narrow.
    B. The "a" sound, as in "a̱ble," "ba̱kery," and "pa̱y." Extended-medium followed by a relaxed-narrow movement.
    C. The "oi" sound, as in "o̱il," "po̱ise," and "enjo̱y." Puckered-wide followed by a relaxed-narrow movement.

BIBLIOGRAPHY

Berg, Frederick S.: *Educational Audiology: Hearing and Speech management.* New York, Grune and Stratton, 1976.

Berg, Frederick S. and Fletcher, Samuel G.: *The hard of Hearing Child.* New York, Grune and Stratton, 1970.

Broberg, Rose F.: *Stories and Games for Easy Lipreading Practice.* Washington, D. C., Volta Bureau, 1972.

Bruhn, Martha: *The Mueller-Walle Method of Lipreading for the Deaf.* Lynn, Massachusetts, Thomas P. Nichols and Sons, 1924.

Bunger, Anna: *Speechreading-Jena Method.* Danville, Illinois, The Interstate Press, 1952.

Butt, D. S. and Chreist, F. M.: A speechreading test for young children. *Volta Review,* 70:225-244, 1968.

Caniglia, Janis: *Apple Tree.* Lake Oswego, Oregon, Dormac Press, 1972.

Fisher, Mae: *Improve Your Lipreading.* Washington, D. C., Volta Bureau, 1974.

Jeffers, Janet and Barley, Margaret: *Speechreading (Lipreading).* Springfield, Illinois, Charles C Thomas, 1971.

Kinzie, Cora and Kinzie, Rose: *Lipreading for Deafened Adults.* Seattle, Washington, 1929.

——— *Lipreading for Children (Book I, II, and III).* Seattle, Washington, 1936.

Lee, Laura: *Developmental Sentence Analysis.* Evanston, Illinois, Northwestern University Press, 1974.

Ling, Daniel: *Speech and the Hearing Impaired Child: Theory and Practice.* Washington, D. C., The Alexander Graham Bell Association for the Deaf, Inc., 1976.

Ling, Daniel and Ling, Agnes H.: *Aural Habilitation: The Foundations of Verbal Learning in Hearing Impaired Children.* Washington, D. C., The Alexander Graham Bell Association for the Deaf, Inc., 1978.

MacNutt, Ena G.: *Hearing With Our Eyes,* Washington, D. C., Volta Bureau, 1953.

Newby Hayes A.: *Audiology,* 4th ed., Englewood Cliffs, New Jersey, Prentice-Hall, Inc., 1979.

Nitchie, Edward: *Lipreading-Principles and Practices.* New York, Frederick A. Stokes, 1912.

Nitchie, Elizabeth: *New Lessons in Lipreading.* Philadelphia, J. B. Lippincott Company, 1950.

Oyer, Herbert J.: *Auditory Communication for the Hard of Hearing.* Englewood Cliffs, New Jersey, Prentice-Hall, Inc., 1966.

The Real Mother Goose. Chicago, Illinois, Rand McNally Co., 1974.

Ross, Mark: *Principles of Aural Rehabilitation.* New York, The Bobbs-Merrill Co., Inc., 1972.

Sanders, Derek A.: *Aural Rehabilitation.* Englewood Cliffs, New Jersey, Prentice-Hall, Inc., 1971.

Streng, Alice: *Hearing Therapy for Children,* 2nd ed., New York, Grune and Stratton, 1969.

Utley, Jean: A test of lipreading ability. *Journal of Speech Disorders, 11*:109-116, 1946.

INDEX

A

Alcorn, K., 7
Alcorn, S., 7
Apple Tree, 127
Auditory Training,
  current methods, 8-11
  exercises, 14, 15, 16-20, 21-123, 124-126
  methods (*see* methods)
  older methods, 6, 7
  plans, 15, 16, 124-126
  speech, use of, 10
Avondino, J., 7

B

Barley, M., 5, 7, 12, 13
Berg, F. S., 8, 9, 10
Brauckmann, K., 3
Breshanan. M., 6
Broberg, R. F., 7
Bruhn, M. E., 3, 5
Bunger, A. M., 3
Butt, D. S., 127

C

Central Institute for the Deaf, 6
Clues
  auditory, 10
  pictures, 19
  sentences, 19
  visual, 10
  words, 6, 8, 18, 19
Cue
  place, 9
  tactile, 9, 16, 17, 18, 19
Cued Speech, 11

D

Data collection, 127-128

form, 128
  tracking responses, 127
Developmental Sentence
  scoring, 127
DiCarlo, L. M., 7
Distinctive features, 15, 19, 126

E

Exercises
  additional, 124-126
  developing, 12-15
  procedures, 16-20

F

Fisher, M., 7
Fletcher, S. G., 8

G

Goldstein, Dr. M., 6
Guberina, P., 9

H

Hearing,
  residual, 6, 10, 13, 16, 124
Hearing aids
  F. M. transmission, 13, 14
  Phonic Ear, 14
  SUVAG, I, II, Mini, 9, 10
  wearable, 14
Hogan, Sister J. L., 9
Homophenous, 3, 4, 8, 13, 15, 17, 18, 124, 125, 142-144

I

Interviews
  adult, 129
  children, 139

J

Jeffers, J., 5, 7, 12-13

K

Kelly, J. C., 7
Kinzie, C. E., 3-5
Kinzie, R., 3-5

L

Larson, L. L., 6
Lee, L., 127
Lesson plans
additional, 124-126
adult, 87-123
developing, 12-15
preschool, 21-29
procedures, 16-20
school age, 30-86
Ling, D., 10
Lowell, E., 7

M

MacNutt, E. G., 7
Methods, Auditory Training
Acoustic Method, 6
Avondino, 7
Babbling Method, 7
Clinician's Handbook for Auditory Training, 7
Consonant Sound Discrimination and Recordings for Auditory Training, 6
Hearing Rehabilitation Children's Series, 6
Let's Listen Records, 6
Play It by Ear, 7
A Manual for Auditory Training, 7
Tadoma Method, 7
Tim and His Hearing Aid, 7
Verbotonal Approach, 9
We Speak Through Music, 6
What's Its Name, 6
Whitehurst Material, 7
Methods, Speechreading
Jena Method, 3, 4, 5
Kinzie Method, 3, 4, 5
Lipreading for Children (Book I, II, and III) 4, 5
Lipreading-Principles and Practices, 4
Mueller-Walle Method, 3, 5, 3-6, 11, 13
Nitchie Method, 4, 5

N

Newby, H. A., 6
Nitchie, E. B., 3

O

Oyer, H. J., 6, 7

P

Porter, A. M., 7
Pronovost, W., 6

Q

Quick Identification Exercises, 12, 13, 16-20, 30-123, 124-126
Quick Recognition Exercises, 12, 13, 16-20, 21-123, 124-126

R

Reighard, J., 3
Ronnei, E. C., 7
Ross, M., 10

S

Sentence Exercises, 12, 13, 16-20, 21-123, 124-126
Sign Language, 13, 16-20
Speechreading
Additional plans, 124-126
Lipreading, 10
Methods (*see* Methods)
Older materials (*see* Methods)
Procedures, 16-20
Tests (*see* Tests)
Speech Sounds,
Visible components, of 142-144
Stoner, M., 7
Story Exercises, 12, 13, 16-20, 21-123, 124-126
Streng, A., 3, 4, 6, 7, 8, 13, 125

T

Tactile, 9, 16, 17, 18, 19
Tests, Speechreading
 Adult, 127
 Children, 127
 Developmental Sentence Scoring, use of, 127
Pre-test — *Apple Tree*, use of, 127
Total Communication, 3, 8, 10, 11, 13, 21

Procedure, 16-20

U

Utley, J., 6, 127

W

Wedenberg, E., 8
Whitaker, B. L., 3
Whitehurst, M., 6, 7